Bible Lives

Jonathan Magonet

SCM PRESS Ltd

For Doro, Gavriel and Abigail

ISBN 0 334 00102 1

First published 1992

by SCM Press Ltd
26–30 Tottenham Road, London N1 4BZ

Typeset at The Spartan Press Ltd, Lymington, Hants
and printed in Finland by
Werner Söderström Oy

Contents

Preface

When I started writing this book I thought of a cartoon by Jules Feiffer. It was one of his usual talking heads, an intellectual book critic writing a review of – the Bible. I don't remember the details. I'm sure the critic praised the author's spare narrative style, rich cast of characters and passionate poetry. He may also have complained about a certain unevenness in the writing – the descriptions of the animals to be sacrificed for different cultic infringements, and perhaps also the rather mundane list of Proverbs, hardly rising to the heights of, for example, the tragic end of King Saul. Nevertheless, the critic concluded, it was a very promising first effort and he looked forward to author's next book.

Second books seem to be harder than the first one. Having poured so much of oneself into the first, the second requires a different sort of discipline. And expectations are higher from those who enjoyed the first. To attempt a second anything seems to be a somewhat masochistic exercise.

Nevertheless the success of *A Rabbi's Bible* (SCM Press 1991) encouraged me to take the risk of having another go. I also wanted to respond to the suggestion of one reviewer that I should concentrate on the exegesis of particular texts. But what texts? The answer seemed to be to develop the series of short pieces called 'Bible Lives' that I wrote over a period of years in the eighties for the London *Jewish Chronicle* – to build the book around biblical characters and the particular texts in which their stories were embedded. Hence 'Bible Lives' – which was always intended as a kind of pun as well, the Bible itself still 'lives'.

I am grateful to the *Jewish Chronicle* for permission to reproduce them here in amended versions and particularly thankful to Meir Persoff who oversaw the series in its original form.

The three longer pieces began life as lectures that were subsequently published: 'Abraham' ('Abraham and God'), 'Esther' ('The Liberal and the Lady') in *Judaism* and 'Jonah' ('"Whither Shall I Go From Your Spirit"; a Study of the book of Jonah') as a pamphlet for the Analytical Psychology Club. The latter piece also had a further existence as an appendix to the second edition of my book *Form and Meaning*, a study of the literary structure of the Book of Jonah, published by Almond Press, Sheffield. I am grateful for permission to reproduce them here again in somewhat amended forms.

I owe the possibility of writing the book to a 'mini-sabbatical', a three month stint as a guest professor at the Kirchliche Hochschule in Wuppertal during the summer semester of 1992. I am particularly grateful to the Ephorus, Siggy Kunath, for the invitation and for the enormous trouble that he and his colleagues, particularly Professors Berthold Klappert and Klaus Haacker, took to look after me during my stay. Though I had much of the material already available in its original form, I needed the time and space to think through how to re-write and re-organize it to fit the new framework.

I owe a debt of gratitude to my colleagues at Leo Baeck College for allowing me to disappear again leaving them to hold the fort: in particular Joanna Weinberg for standing in for my duties as Principal and John Olbrich for keeping the administration going without my daily interference!

I am grateful to John Bowden of SCM Press for accepting my first book so readily and giving me the green light to try a second one, which I hope will fit into their growing Jewish list.

Above all, as with my last book, I want to thank my wife Dorothea and my children Gavriel and Abigail for allowing me to disappear yet again for an extended period, so soon after my last long absence in Israel. Without their loving support, nothing would have been possible.

Introduction

I remember a discussion with a Rabbinic colleague who was reviewing a new book on the Bible. It was written from a psychological perspective and he was most irritated with it. 'How can you psychoanalyse the figure of Abraham in the Bible when the stories all come from different sources!?'

I can understand his annoyance. Having committed himself to source criticism it was difficult to have some newer critics trampling all over the theory and reading the texts as a 'unity', let alone unleashing psychology on them.

Yet, having been committed to a literary approach to the Hebrew Bible for years I find myself particularly interested in where the line can be drawn in such an exercise.

The biblical narratives work too well. They are often tantalizing in their brevity and give the most sparing details of the characters they portray, yet we find ourselves with little difficulty filling in the details out of our own imagination. A few lines can sketch out a total personality, or describe an entire lifetime. They can also leave us thrashing about in bewilderment trying to figure out what is really going on, who is really acting upon whom – and also how far events are only being conducted on a human plane, and how far the hand of God is at least manipulating the scenery, if not the actual players. All this made more difficult because of how little we know of the social, religious and political milieu in which so much of it was written and indeed of the intended audience.

The challenge therefore, at least in the shorter pieces here, was to see how far it was possible to go in analysing a character by just using the minimal information available in the Hebrew text. Sometimes I have gone further afield in the Bible for essential background information, but I hope that I have avoided cheating in the description of character itself. Sometimes, as a sort of appendix, I have added Rabbinic insights for additional colouring.

For conceiving the structure of this book I owe a debt to the memory of the late Pearl Bailey. Pearl had an amazing career with international success as a singer, comedienne, dramatic actress and film star. But she was also one of the greatest ambassadors of America (literally at one stage speaking on the floor of the UN). As a world traveller she became a friend to thousands of people through her public performances and to innumerable individuals because of the love she was able to give and receive.

But my particular debt to her comes from a different aspect of her story. She had a heart attack following which she was clinically dead for a few moments. On recovery she became deeply interested in religion, and, never one to do things by halves, she enrolled in a university in the States and took a degree in Theology. So while doing a stint in London at the Talk of the Town, she decided to pursue her studies, and took courses during her spare time at Leo Baeck College.

Pearl studying was still Pearl – which meant that she did a lot of the talking, overflowing with anecdotes and experiences of her own, but she could also listen and was quick to pick up ideas. It was my task to teach her a little Bible, and given her show business background, it made sense to introduce her to a celebrated biblical 'performance', the famous 'Song of the Vineyard' in Isaiah chapter 5.

We read through it, and I explained how the prophet sets up his listeners by telling them a parable about his friend who had a vineyard. How his friend chose the most fertile ground, cleared it of stones, dug it up, picked the best possible vine and planted it. But to his surprise, instead of yielding perfect grapes it produced rotten ones. Now the prophet turns to his listeners and asks them to judge between his friend and this rotten vine – didn't he do everything possible for it? When his listeners agree, the prophet tells how his friend will now uproot everything that he has planted – and then, as they nod in agreement, he hits them with the message of his parable. That they, the listeners, are the vine that God has planted, and their rotten behaviour means that God has to destroy them.

Pearl's response was totally unexpected. 'That's just like my cabaret act! First you sing them a fast number to get their attention. Then a slower one. Then you talk to them a little just to keep them interested, and hit them again with something fast.' That may not be the exact order she gave, but she had clearly got the point, and I also saw that Isaiah text in a completely new way. That intimacy she got with her audience was choreographed, but in no way artificial – she earned the love we all gave her.

When organizing the structure of this book I thought of Pearl, and tried to pace it. So I will be running a number of the shorter pieces, then a longer one, then some shorter ones, hopefully to keep the whole thing moving. I have no idea if such a technique works as a book, but maybe Pearl would have liked it.

And having mentioned her I can't help adding one other thing she taught me which gives just another hint of her craftmanship. When you're playing with a band, she said, you have to keep a conversation going with them and bring them along with you as well. Otherwise they get bored and go off and do their own thing. There are singers who only play to the audience and ignore the band – you can always tell if you look at what is going on behind the singer's back. So in that sense a performance is actually a meeting between the singer and the band, and the audience is a privileged eavesdropper on that conversation. Such a performance is therefore a double-sided encounter and it is a measure of Pearl's genius that she managed to pull it off in both directions.

Does that say anything to the way we read the Bible? Maybe. Because though we interpret it for ourselves and our own contemporary 'audience', we have still to be true to the text itself, to talk *to* it, and not just *about* it – or it might also get bored with us. Perhaps that's another explanation of the Rabbinic idea that 'the text never loses its plain meaning', however fanciful or important the interpretation we give it. We have to respect the source of our music if we want to play for others.

There is a small group of pieces towards the end of the book that are somewhat different from the others. Some of the pieces for the *Jewish Chronicle* were scheduled to coincide with the festival of Purim, which is a sort of Jewish version of Carnival. On that day all usual formalities and conventions are overturned, including the way we read and study Torah, the teaching of God. Parodies of Rabbinic teachings abound for this day, so it seemed appropriate to produce, as a 'Purim-spiel', some sort of spoof biblical exegesis. I include some specimens here – for light relief, but also because humour is an essential part of Jewish self-understanding and life.

In the case of On ben Pelet, one of my favourite biblical characters, there are two versions included. The shorter one was aimed at the

Jewish Chronicle readership, but the other was a sort of private joke at the expense of my fellow biblical exegetes.

Some technical matters. Most of the time I have referred to 'the Bible', rather than speak of 'the Old Testament', which is problematic for Jews (for us it is not 'Old', nor is there a 'New' Testament to replace it), or 'the Hebrew Bible', which is perhaps a more accurate term but a little tedious to write every time.

Since it is impossible to find an appropriate word to designate God that accurately reflects the complex possibilities of understanding the Hebrew term usually translated as 'Lord', I have settled for 'Eternal' – and will explain a bit more about the meaning of some of the names in the chapter on Balaam.

For the purpose of transliteration of Hebrew words I have used 'ch' (as pronounced in the Scottish 'loch') to designate the Hebrew letter '*kaf*'. I have usually used the letter 'h' to designate both the letter 'hey' and 'het', but for the latter I have occasionally used 'ch' as well. A certain inconsistency is inevitable as some Hebrew words are more familiar and certain spellings are in regular use. As always, I hope that readers will want to familiarize themselves with the original Hebrew so that this dimension of the Bible is opened up to them.

While working on the stories I became aware of how many names appear and of how difficult it is at times to keep them all in our head. This is especially the case today when Bible stories, their plots and characters, are no longer a major part of our general culture. Once or twice the number of names that appear, just to give a background to a piece, can be a bit overwhelming. But one aim of this exercise is to bring to centre stage precisely some of the less well-known figures, so please persevere!

Part of the fun of writing these sketches in the first place was the detective work of finding as many relevant clues as possible to the personality or history of the particular character and then composing a consistent picture. But in reworking them and putting this collection together I have become conscious of another aim: to encourage the readers to want to go back to the text for themselves and check out (or challenge!) my interpretations. In that way we may come to share in that experience already recorded by one of the anonymous contributors to the poetry of the Psalms:

Open my eyes that I may see wondrous things out of Your Torah. (Ps. 119.18)

1

Heroines and Heroes

SHIPHRAH AND PUAH

Perhaps the most striking feature of the beginning of the Book of Exodus is the enormous significance it places upon a handful of women. With the exception of two of them they are unnamed. The mother of Moses and his sister are given names, but only later in the book – perhaps because the telling of the story is so urgent, the birth and growth of Moses so important, that there is no time to stop and mention names – because, as is shown in Exodus 6, once you start to mention Moses' relatives, the whole family tree has to be added.

The case of the daughter of Pharaoh is different. She is never named, presumably because her rank is significant enough and raises a whole range of fascinating questions about what could have prompted her to adopt a Hebrew child against the express wishes of her father. In the Rabbinic tradition, however, she is identified a bit more precisely because of a mysterious comment in the Book of Chronicles. I Chronicles 4.18 makes a cryptic reference to one Bitya daughter of Pharaoh whom Mered married. Clearly, in the Rabbinic view, this had to be the same woman who saved Moses, who therefore subsequently cast in her lot with the Israelites and left Egypt with them. But how does she acquire the name 'Bitya', 'daughter of Yah', the latter being another name for Israel's God? Because God renamed her: 'Since you took one of My sons as your own, I will "adopt" you as my daughter!'

But two women are named, Shiphrah and Puah, the two 'Hebrew midwives'. Perhaps in some ways they are the most significant in the entire story because without them nothing would have been possible at all. Their refusal to carry out

Pharaoh's secret plan of genocide was a magnificent act of resistance against an unjust order, and indeed against the whole apparatus of state power. On all accounts their names deserve to be preserved and their story told. But how did they get away with it?

Pharaoh gives them his instructions, an indication of the secrecy that is to surround these murders:

> When you are present at the birth of the Hebrew women, look upon the 'stones' – if it is a son, then kill it, but if it is a daughter she shall live. But the midwives feared God and did not do as the King of Egypt said, and they let the boys live (or 'helped sustain them') (Ex. 1.16–17).

The reference to this sentence in their orders coming from the 'King of Egypt' emphasizes that he represented the supreme authority of their society and so reinforces our recognition of their courage in defying him.

The text says that they 'feared God', but it is important to note what this might mean in a biblical context. When Abraham visits Gerar he pretends that his wife Sarah is his sister. When King Abimelech takes her and later discovers the truth he asks Abraham why he deceived him. Abraham's answer is that he was afraid there was no 'fear of God' in that place (Gen. 20.11). When the Egyptian magicians try to reproduce the plagues sent by God and finally cannot, they give up by pointing out that it is 'the finger of God' at work (Ex. 8.15). However, in both cases the use of the word 'God' may indeed be meant to refer to the 'Divinity', or, instead, imply some more general idea about the 'natural order' that operates within the world. The magicians were actually saying that the plague was something quite outside the realm of 'magic' in which they operated – it was precisely what insurance policies call 'an act of God', by which is meant a 'natural disaster'. Likewise in the case of Abimelech's society, Abraham was saying that there was no 'rule of law', no 'moral order' in the land, so he knew that people would misbehave. So it is a question as to whether the midwives were literally 'God-fearing' women in the specific sense of being believers and motivated on religious grounds, or that they had a strong natural sense of justice and a moral code. In either event they acted out of deeply held convictions.

So the 'King of Egypt', again in his full authority, summoned the midwives to give an accounting. The text tells us that they replied to

'Pharaoh', which makes us wonder if there is some implication in this change of designation. They said:

> But these Hebrews are not like Egyptian women, for they are 'lively'. Before the midwives come to them they have given birth! (Ex. 1.19).

There are a number of innuendos in their reply. The Egyptians they mention are referred to as 'women', the 'Hebrews' are not dignified with such a title – 'they are not like our (refined) Egyptian ladies!'. Instead they are 'lively', *hayot*, an unusual form of the verb meaning 'to be' or 'to live'. But the form in the Hebrew is almost identical with the word for 'animals', *hayyot*, so that it is possible that Pharaoh was meant to hear behind their words yet another expression of contempt. They go on to explain that these women are so 'animal-like', that before the midwife can get there, they have 'dropped' the baby. Because of that, runs the argument, we cannot discreetly kill the male babies at the moment they are born when no one would notice.

All of their explanations feed on Pharaoh's prejudices, to reinforce the idea that they were doing their best in very trying circumstances. Perhaps that is why he is addressed as 'Pharaoh'; not the 'King of Egypt', but the hater of the descendants of Jacob. 'What are we supposed to do with these "creatures" ', they plead, 'you know what they're like! It is certainly not our fault!'

Till now Pharaoh's tactics have been covert. His plan depended on the secret activity of the midwives at the birth. But now, perhaps, he feels sufficiently confident to act more openly – and the order goes out to the entire people to throw every male child into the Nile (1.22).

The midwives are not forgotten by God, though it is not entirely clear from the text what was their reward:

> God did well by the midwives, and the people multiplied and grew greatly. Because the midwives feared God, He made for *them* houses (1.20–21).

The problem is in the word 'them' in the second sentence which is actually in a masculine form, when we would expect it to be 'feminine', referring to the 'midwives'. It could be that the two verses are meant to be parallel statements, the first half of each talking about the midwives, but the second half about the children of Israel, so that the Israelites were the ones who had 'houses'. This would actually fit in with the beginning of the chapter which records how the children of 'Israel' came down to Egypt with Jacob their father, each man with his 'house' (1.1). So it was the children of Israel whose households multiplied. Despite all of Pharaoh's attempts, Jacob's descendants continued to increase as God's blessing to Abraham had promised, and as the chapter had already indicated (Ex. 1.7).

The more common view is that, despite the odd grammar, the sentence refers to the midwives. Not only did God reward them (v. 3), but also built for them 'houses', that is, their own 'dynasties'.

But this brings us back to the problem faced already by the Rabbis. Were Shiphrah and Puah Egyptian women or Hebrews? The phrase 'Hebrew Midwives', in the Hebrew, can be read in either way: they could be Midwives who were themselves 'Hebrew', or 'Midwives *to* the Hebrews' who could belong to any nation.

This raises further problems, because though midwives who were Egyptian might be counted on to obey orders from the King of Egypt himself, how could Hebrew women possibly carry out such an act of murder on the children of their own people? Nevertheless Rashi, the great mediaeval Jewish commentator, following an earlier Rabbinic tradition, identifies them as Jochebed and Miriam, respectively Moses' mother and sister.

But irrespective of their precise identity, their courage in disobeying the order to commit murder makes them the earliest, and in some ways the most powerful, examples of resistance to an evil regime. For their generosity of spirit, love of life and resourcefulness they deserve that their names be recorded and remembered: Shiphrah and Puah, the midwives who helped bring into the world a generation of living children and the great biblical movement for human freedom.

RITZPAH

Sometimes the first appearance of people in the Bible leaves us quite unprepared for what will happen to them later. After the death of King Saul, David consolidated his hold on the south of the country, establishing his kingdom in Hebron over the house of Judah.

In the north, Saul's former commander-in-chief, Abner, had taken Saul's son, Ishbosheth, under his protection and set him up as king over the rest of the country. From the biblical account,

Ishbosheth appears to have been a weak man, and Abner was literally the power behind the throne.

Their relationship seems to have been strained, but matters came to a head when Ishbosheth accused Abner of having an affair with his father's concubine, Ritzpah (II Sam. 3.6–7). So we first meet her as a woman who once loved a king and is now caught up in the political squabbling over the succession to the throne.

Although Ishbosheth's objections may have been a personal concern about Ritzpah, or a feeling about the respect due to his father's memory, there is an underlying political dimension to this accusation. For the acquiring of the concubine of the former king somehow symbolized the transfer of the power of that king to his successor.

So, later on, Absalom was to take David's concubines as an indication of his bid for power (II Sam. 16.21–22), and to burn his own bridges in his relations with his father. And Adonijah was put to death by his brother, Solomon, for similarly wishing to marry Abishag, the last woman to share David's bed (I Kings 2.17–25).

In the subsequent argument between Abner and Ishbosheth (II Sam. 3.6–11), Abner made his final break with the house of Saul and transferred his allegiance to David, setting in motion the steps that would lead to David's rule over the united kingdom – and, incidentally, Abner's own death at the hand of David's commander-in-chief, Joab.

To these palace struggles Ritzpah is both a witness and passive participant. What her feelings about Saul were are not related, nor whether she even had a relationship with Abner – all we have from the record is Ishbosheth's accusation and Abner's angry but evasive reply:

> Am I a dog's head of Judah? This day I keep showing loyalty to the house of Saul, your father, to his brothers and to his friends, and have not given you into the hand of David, and yet you charge me today with a fault concerning a woman! (II Sam. 3.8).

Of Ritzpah's subsequent situation we know nothing. With Abner's death she presumably lost her protector and either stayed on in the north while the kingdom lasted or came under David's sphere of influence.

But nothing we know of her prepares us for her second appearance at the other end of the Second Book of Samuel, in an incident that is difficult to date, but which probably occurred early in David's reign over all Israel.

The story (in II Sam. 21.1–14) is another of those ambiguous situations that continually force us to reassess David's political actions. After a three-year famine, David sought the explanation from God and learned that it was caused by an act of Saul that had not been set right.

The event concerned the Gibeonites, local Canaanite people who had tricked Joshua into sparing them at the time of the conquest and who became Israel's 'hewers of wood and drawers of water' (Josh. 9.3–27). Some of them had been killed by Saul 'because of his zeal for the children of Israel and Judah'.

For killing their people, the Gibeonites demanded from David the death of seven of Saul's sons. David spared Jonathan's son because of the covenant he had made with him while still fleeing from Saul; and Ishbosheth had meanwhile been assassinated.

So the two sons of Ritzpah and the five sons of Merab, Saul's daughter, were handed over to the Gibeonites who hanged them 'at the beginning of the barley harvest'.

Though the story is told in terms of a crime being put right, and is an uncomfortable reminder that God calls Israel to account for her treatment of other peoples who live in her midst, the event also rid David of the last danger of a claim to the throne from Saul's descendants. Once again David has managed to do the 'right thing', but incidentally advance his own cause.

The Gibeonites demanded that the bodies remain hanging, something forbidden in Deuteronomy 21.22–3, and they stayed there 'from the beginning of the harvest till rain fell upon them from the heavens', signalling the end of the drought.

> But Ritzpah, the daughter of Aiah, took sackcloth, and spread it for herself on the rock . . . and she did not allow the birds of the air to come upon them by day or the beasts of the field by night (II Sam. 21.10).

This extraordinary, tragic vigil galvanized David into action. He gathered the bones of Saul and Jonathan from the men of Jabesh-Gilead who had rescued the corpses from the Philistines, added to them the bodies of the seven dead grandsons and finally laid them all to rest in the land of Benjamin, in Zela, in the tomb of Kish, Saul's father.

Who was this extraordinary woman who refused to accept what

was seen as the judgment of God on Saul's issue and possibly risked her life in a dangerous political protest against the decision of the king? She lost her sons, but won for them at least an honourable burial.

Her dark tortured figure, defying sleep, fighting against the wild beasts and carrion birds before the decaying bodies of her children, haunts us. She appears at the other end of the Books of Samuel from Hannah, the other 'mother in Israel' who shaped history through her love, courage and devotion.

But Ritzpah is every mother who sees her sons killed before their time for reasons of state, be they in time of peace or in war. All that remains for her is to preserve the dignity of their memory and live on to bear witness and call to account the rulers of the world.

ZIPPORAH

She enters the scene in one of the classical hero tales. The exiled Moses, fleeing for his life from Egypt, arrives in the land of Midian. He settles by the well, the centre of community life and, as in other biblical episodes (see the chapter on 'Eliezer'), the place where the hero will find his bride.

There is a priest of Midian, Jethro his name. For some reason, never revealed, his status does not afford him the respect and protection one might assume. When his seven daughters come to water their sheep, shepherds chase them away. 'So Moses arose and saved them and watered their flock' (Ex. 2.17).

When Jethro is introduced in person, there may be a touch of crude humour intended. For the biblical world, the number seven has great significance, and in a patriarchal society sons are considered the great blessing. When the women of Bethlehem wish to give Ruth the ultimate praise, they describe her as being 'better than seven sons' (Ruth 4.15). In trying to reassure his barren wife Hannah of his love despite her childlessness, Elkanah tells her that he is better for her than even ten sons (I Sam. 1.8) – which is well-intentioned but, in the circumstances, perhaps a little tactless. However, when Hannah finally gives birth to Samuel, her song of triumph also celebrates how God has made 'the barren woman bear seven' (I Sam. 2.5).

However, in such a world, as in later folklore, the man with seven daughters, for whom he must find husbands, may be seen as a figure

of fun. Hence the urgency of Jethro's reaction to his daughters'
story that an Egyptian man had rescued them, drawn from the well
and watered the sheep.

But where is he?! Why have you left the gentleman?! Call him
and let him eat bread! (Ex. 2.20).

It may even be that this simple invitation to eat bread is actually a
euphemism. 'Eating bread' has sexual connotations in the story of
Joseph and Potiphar's wife. Genesis 39.6 refers to Joseph's status in
Potiphar's household:

He left everything that was his in the hand of Joseph and
concerned himself with nothing *except the bread that he ate . . .*

When Joseph is trying to resist the advances of Potiphar's wife,
Joseph similarly describes his situation, but parallel to the phrase
about 'the bread that he ate' we find:

No one has a more important position in this household than me
and he (Potiphar) *has not withheld anything from me except you,
for you are his wife* (Gen. 39.9).

Even more explicit about equating eating with sexual behaviour
is the somewhat misogynous statement in Proverbs 30.20:

This is the way of the adulterous woman: She eats, wipes her
mouth and says, 'I never did anything!'.

In any event, Zipporah emerges from amongst the seven
daughters of Jethro to become Moses' wife and the mother of his
two sons, born in exile. Between this appearance and her next, the
event at the burning bush transforms the nature and meaning of
Moses' life.

Despite his objections and evasion, he is charged with returning
to Egypt to be God's instrument in rescuing the Children of Israel.
He requests permission from Jethro to leave, and departs, taking
with him his wife and sons.

Into this simple journey erupts one of the most shocking and
bewildering events in the Hebrew Bible. The brief narrative both
reveals and conceals what occurs.

At a lodging place on the way, the Eternal met him and sought to
kill him. Then Zipporah took a flint and cut off the foreskin of her
son, touched it to his feet and said: 'Surely you are my

bridegroom of blood.' So He let him alone. Then she said: 'A bridegroom of blood because of the circumcision' (Ex. 4.24–26).

There are several problems of interpretation here because the language is very unclear about who is doing what to whom. Who is it that God attacks, Moses or one of his two sons? Zipporah touched the foreskin of her son to 'his' feet – whose? Even the word 'feet' is not altogether clear since it can mean any part of the leg region from the toes to the genitalia.

The mysterious phrase, 'A bridegroom of blood' may have been associated with the ceremony of circumcision, but has no echo elsewhere in the Bible. Does it belong to Zipporah's Midianite tradition?

But beyond even the basic language problems are far more puzzling ones. Why should God wish to kill Moses (or one of his sons) when he is actually embarking on the mission? Why is Moses not active in the subsequent events? What led Zipporah to circumcise her son and then touch his or Moses' 'feet' with the foreskin?

Even if God's seeking to 'kill' Moses is only a biblical way of saying Moses became severely ill; even if it was because he had failed to circumcise his son before he set off and was therefore being punished; even if the whole episode prefigures later events: the killing of the firstborn of Egypt, the blood on the doorposts of Israelite houses during that night, the times in the wilderness when God struck the Israelites and even Moses – with all these possible explanations it remains a dark, frightening event: the night visit of death, a shedding of blood, a mysterious ritual and incantation that turns the threat aside.

If Zipporah had not had the secret knowledge or intuition or initiative to act, the biblical story might have ended there with Moses' mysterious death.

Unlike the courage of the other women who feature so prominently in the early chapters of the Book of Exodus, the midwives (see the chapter on Shiphrah and Puah), the good nature of Pharaoh's daughter and the resourcefulness of Moses' sister, Zipporah evokes utterly different powers, quite beyond the rational forces the Bible usually acknowledges and values.

Perhaps that is why all is not revealed, but neither is the tale concealed. We are left to imagine and conjure our own solutions.

Is this the last we hear of Zipporah? She will rejoin Moses again at

Sinai, having been staying with her father, though it is not at all clear when, as the text casually informs us, Moses had 'sent her away' (Ex. 18.2). But is she also the 'Cushite woman' about whom Miriam and Aaron speak in a later episode (Num. 12), for a 'Cushite' would be black and there is nothing to suggest that the Midianite Zipporah was black.

Presumably she lived out her days and died as the honoured wife of Moses, but in the vast sweep of events this detail required no special mention. Yet this daughter of the priest of Midian retains her own mysterious power quite apart from the stature of her husband to whom she was also wedded by a knife of flint and the strange healing power of ritual, incantation and blood.

JEPHTHAH

Jephthah the Gileadite, one of the judges from the period before Israel had a king, is known to history, if he is remembered at all, as the man who sacrificed his daughter.

The story from the Book of Judges 11 is briefly told. Jephthah fought the Ammonites and made a vow to God that if he succeeded, he would sacrifice the first thing to leave his house to greet him when he returned home. He won a great victory and the first to come out to meet him was his daughter!

The possibility that a father could offer up his child is familiar to us from the story of the binding of Isaac, Genesis 22, though there the child was spared. (We will have to look at that story in the chapter on Abraham.) But what motivated a man like Jephthah to make such a rash vow? Let's look at the text in greater detail.

Jephthah the Gileadite was a great warrior, but he was the son of a prostitute, his father being Gilead. Gilead's real wife bore him sons, and when his wife's sons grew up, they threw Jephthah out, saying to him: 'You will not inherit anything in our father's house for you are the son of that other woman!'

Jephthah fled from his brothers and lived in the land of Tov, and there gathered round Jephthah worthless men who went out raiding with him.

Some time later the Ammonites went to war against Israel. When the Ammonites attacked Israel, the elders of Gilead went to bring Jephthah back from the land of Tov. They said to Jephthah: 'Come and be our commander so that we can fight the

Ammonites.' But Jephthah said to the elders of Gilead: 'Aren't you the ones who rejected me and threw me out of my father's house? Why are you coming to me now when you are in trouble?'

The elders of Gilead replied to Jephthah: 'But that is why we have come back to you now. Go with us so that we can fight the Ammonites, then you shall be the leader of all the inhabitants of Gilead.' (Judg. 11.1–8).

At first glance, the arguments of the elders and Jephthah seem straightforward: the elders are in need, Jephthah is rightly resentful. But there is a hidden agenda to their discussions.

At the end of the previous chapter we have had a brief notice about the war begun by the Ammonites and the discussions that then took place (10.18).

Then the troops, the officers of Gilead, said to one another: 'Let the man who is the first to fight the Ammonites be the leader of all the inhabitants of Gilead.'

In their private discussions, or even as a public announcement, the generals had agreed to appoint such a person as *rosh* (literally, 'head'), 'leader' of Gilead. But in their offer to Jephthah the elders, that is to say, the political leaders, who often have a different agenda from the military, had asked him to become *katzin*, a broad term for leadership, often with a military sense. Presumably the elders still thought of him as unworthy to be the head of their society because of his origins.

So, behind their suggestion is an internal disagreement between the military and political leadership about what precisely is on offer, and Jephthah's refusal may also be a negotiating ploy; he is holding out for full recognition. Certainly, that is how the elders seem to understand it, for in their reply they make a better offer and now speak of his becoming the *rosh*, their leader.

Jephthah accepts and reveals another side of his character (v. 9):

If you bring me back to fight the Ammonites, and if the Eternal delivers them to me, then I shall be your leader (*rosh*).

The elders agree and in a public ceremony they officially appoint him (v. 11). Here we should note a nuance in the Hebrew. The word *am*, is usually translated as 'people' (God refers to Israel as *ammi*, 'My people'), but quite often it has the more limited sense of 'citizens army', and this is how I have understood it above (10.18), 'the troops'. So in verse 11, where the word appears again, we have to decide whether it is 'the people (of Gilead)' as a whole who elect Jephthah to his post, or the same 'troops' that decided what the post should be.

> Then Jephthah went with the elders of Gilead and the 'people/ army' appointed him as leader (*rosh*) and commander (*katzin*) over them. And Jephthah spoke all his terms before the Eternal at Mitzpah.

Jephthah has won his fight for recognition in his society, but he also marks the occasion with a religious ceremony. We cannot tell whether he does this as a further political move to reinforce his appointment, or because he is a genuinely religious man who recognizes in this turn of events the hand of God.

Certainly, as the story shows, the spirit of the Eternal comes upon him and he was successful in his fight. On the eve of the battle he makes his famous vow (v. 30):

> If You will give the Ammonites into my hand, then whatever first comes out from the doors of my house to greet me on my safe return from the Ammonites, that one shall belong to the Eternal and I will offer it up as a burnt offering.

The language of the vow is imprecise and seems to suggest he had an animal in mind. But why did he do it?

In some way, it is an expression of piety, but it is also an attempt to manipulate God. It is as if too much were at stake for him at this crucial moment. The outcast son had been offered a triumphant return. More important than the victory over the Ammonites was wiping out the stain on his ancestry, his hurt at being thrown out from his family home and the years he spent in exile. With so much to win, he lost his balance and tried to guarantee success.

In the event, the first to greet him was his daughter. The text tells us specifically that she was his only child, so he loses his chance of a dynasty, of securing a future for his newly restored name.

The Rabbinic tradition did not rate Jephthah's actions too highly. On the whole they disliked the whole idea of vows, perhaps taking their cue from Ecclesiastes.

> When you make a promise to God, do not delay in fulfilling it, for God has no pleasure in fools. Whatever you vow fulfil. It is better not to vow than to vow and not fulfil. Let not your mouth cause guilt to your body and plead before the collector 'it was just a

mistake'. Why should God be angry at your speech and destroy what you have achieved? (Eccles. 5.3–5).

The Talmud records the debate between Rabbi Meir and Rabbi Judah:

Rabbi Meir said: Better than those who promise God and do as they promised, or those who promise and do not do as they promised, are those who never promise God anything, but who carry out their religious obligations quietly and faithfully at the appropriate time and in the appropriate way.
    Rabbi Judah disagreed: Best of all are those who make promises to God and keep their promises (*Chullin* 2a).

On this reading Rabbi Judah has a more adventurous view of the service of God than Rabbi Meir. But in the specific case of Jephthah's vow, the Rabbis could not understand why he did not just cancel it when it turned out in this tragic way. After all, in their view, the apparatus existed for the substitution of a monetary payment for a blemished or otherwise inappropriate sacrifice, simply by going to the High Priest. Anyway, they argued, what kind of a vow was it! Anything could have come out of the house to greet him – perhaps a camel, or an ass, or dog, and how could he sacrifice an 'unclean' animal to God! (*Genesis Rabbah* 60.3).
    Why did Jethro not make the substitute payment? They blamed his sense of pride. Not only his but also that of the High Priest, Phinehas. The latter said: 'He needs me, am I to go to him?! Anyhow, I am the High Priest and son of a High Priest, am I supposed to go to such an unlearned man?' And Jephthah said: 'Am I, the chief of Israel's leaders, to go to Phinehas?!' Between the two of them, the girl died (ibid.).
    Since we have tried to read the text closely and pick up any nuances that it may contain, perhaps we should take note of a brilliant observation by Rabbi David Kimchi, (RaDaK) one of the great mediaeval Bible commentators (Provence *c.* 1160 – *c.* 1235). From time to time he brings comments in the name of his father. In this case his father had noted an ambiguity in the Hebrew text of Jephthah's vow. The precise phrase is: *v'hayah l'adonay v'ha'aleitihu olah*, literally 'it shall be to the Eternal *and* I will offer it up as a burnt offering'. The problem lies with the Hebrew letter '*vav*' at the front of the word '*v'ha'aleitihu*' '*and* I will offer it up'. Whereas the '*vav*' most commonly is translated as *and*, it can mean

other things as well, in fact sometimes it merely serves to affect the
grammatical state of the following verb and should not be translated
at all. But one of its meanings is 'or' as, for example, in Exodus
21.15, where the hebrew pair *aviv v'immo*, clearly means 'whoever
strikes his father *or* mother' and not 'father *and* mother'. So Radak
would have us read the text to mean:

> Whatever comes out of my house shall be dedicated to God, or (if
> it is appropriate to be offered as a burnt offering), then I will offer
> it up as a burnt offering.

Radak, still following his father, then explains the somewhat
mysterious conclusion to the chapter.

> She said to her father, 'Do this thing for me: Let me go for two
> months and I will leave and go to the mountains and weep for my
> virginity, I and my companions.' He said, 'Good.' and he sent her
> for two months and she went with her companions and she wept
> over her virginity upon the mountains. Then at the end of two
> months she returned to her father and he did to her according to
> his vow which he had vowed and she did not know (or, had not
> known) a man, and this became a law in Israel: that each year the
> daughters of Israel went to weep for the daughter of Jephthah the
> Gileadite for four days during the year (Judg. 11.37–40).

What is the implication of the phrase 'and she did not know a
man' (or equally possible, 'she had not known a man')? Moreover,
though it says that Jephthah 'did to her according to his vow', it does
not explicitly say that he sacrificed her. According to Radak,
Jephthah dedicated his daughter to God, as one dedicates first fruits
or firstborn animals – that is to say they become the property of God
and are no longer available to the rest of the population. Jephthah
did not sacrifice her but she was forced to remain unmarried and
unable to have children of her own, in effect the first 'nun'.

Apart from being a brilliant reading of the text as it is, this also
solves the mystery of why more is not said about such a scandalous
thing as a child sacrifice. The Bible is rarely coy about mentioning
difficult things, and surely it would have warranted more comment
at the end of the chapter, unless one postulates some sort of later
editing out of the details. But certainly Radak's explanation fits very
well the ethos of the Bible.

If the daughter did not actually die, her sacrifice was no less a
sacrifice, particularly given the importance in a patriarchal society

for a woman to have children. To give up that possibility was a real tragedy.

But to return to Jephthah, the end of his story echoes the beginning, the daughter who remains a virgin standing in stark contrast to the fact that his mother was a prostitute. A psychoanalytic approach to the story could work wonders with this factor. But there is a further dimension that brings a tragic irony to Jephthah's fate. His problem was that he was not accepted as part of his father's family, he had no status within his own society because effectively he had no past. The military needs now offered him the chance to reverse his situation and make him the leader of the very people who had spurned him, hence the urgency of his vow, which was an attempt to force God's hand. But the result was that by losing his daughter's opportunity to have children, he could not build his own family to take forward his new status. In his desire to cancel out his past he cancelled out his future as well.

That should be the end of the story of Jephthah for our purposes, but as so often within the Bible there are wheels within wheels. Jephthah's story does not stand in isolation. Two chapters before it in the Book of Judges is the story of Abimelech which I have treated in my *A Rabbi's Bible*. Briefly, the first six verses of Judges 9 recount Abimelech's rise to power. The parallels to Jephthah are many, and clearly the juxtaposition of the two stories, only a chapter apart, encourages us to compare and contrast them. Abimelech is also the son of 'the other woman', in his case not a prostitute but a Canaanite concubine (Judg. 8.30–31). Though we are not told about how Abimelech's brothers treated him, he is enough of an outsider to plot and achieve the death of sixty-nine out of the seventy of them. He also associates with 'worthless men', a term that requires a bit of explanation. Literally the Hebrew '*reikim*', means 'empty', and presumably it refers to those who are 'landless' and have no real stake in the society. They become outlaws and such people gather around Jephthah, whereas Abimelech actually hires them. Moreover those hired by Abimelech are described not just as 'empty', but also as '*pochazim*', 'restless', 'disturbed', perhaps implying 'violent'.

Whereas Jephthah goes on to become an honoured leader of his people, Abimelech claws his way to power through violence, and his end is also violent. Thus the two stories, side by side, seem to indicate on another level the inner struggle for values that have to take place irrespective of the misfortunes that may attend us. Both are outcasts, and anyway marginal people, one turns destructive the other seeks to serve. Of course it is not that simple, but the juxtaposition of the two stories demands that we examine how the two fates differ.

And just as a final Freudian touch, Abimelech, whose problematic history began with the outsider status of his mother ends up being killed; by a stone dropped on his head from the walls of a city he is besieging – by a woman. Like the story of Jephthah both tales are framed by the impact of women, bound to the protagonists from birth to death, either real or symbolic. I recognize the symmetry, but I have yet to grasp what it might mean.

THE PARTISAN POET

There are many anonymous figures in the Hebrew Bible, incidental characters in stories or background people in a crowd. Few leave a traceable record that allows us to learn a little about the things that moved them or determined the lives they were to lead.

Yet one document has come down to us, a poem of enormous power, that gives some clues to the unknown writer and his world. It is Psalm 137:

> By the rivers of Babylon, there we sat, also we wept, when we remembered Zion.

The author, presumably a man, is identified as one of the Levites who was a musician in the Jerusalem Temple, carried into captivity to Babylon after the conquest of Jerusalem.

There they experienced the taunts of their captors – 'Come musicians, sing us a song!'

> Sing us one of the songs of Zion! (137.3).

On its face value, this could be the taunting of those on guard duty, bored with their tour of duty and looking for something to relieve the tedium. But there may be a more sinister meaning.

For the 'songs of Zion' are the religious hymns and chants of the Temple service. In biblical thought they are the earthly counterpart of the angelic choirs singing their praises to God, as in Isaiah's vision (Isa. 6.3). They are part of the mystery of Israel's cosmic role in proclaiming the unity of God in the world.

On the political level, the destruction of the Temple and the exile of the leadership of Judah represented a defeat for their God in the eyes of the Babylonians – to sing the songs of Zion in exile would mean the acknowledgment by the prisoners of the submission of their God to the conquerors.

Whether on the level of private suffering, or of the wider religious or political significance suggested above, the outraged horror at this request sets an underlying tone of bitterness to the psalm which will surface at the end with its violent concluding curse.

The answer of the psalmist, or of the group of Levites, is an anguished question:

How can we sing the song of the Eternal in a strange land? (137.4).

But this question, which may already be a statement of defiance, leads into one of the most famous passages in the Bible.

From speaking of 'we', the subject becomes the 'I' of the psalmist himself. Instead of singing of 'Zion', which usually means, in the Book of Psalms, the spiritual centre of Israel's faith, he recalls 'Jerusalem', which implies both the spiritual and political capital of the nation.

It is as if he is saying: You want to hear a religious song to indicate our submission? Well, I am afraid I cannot oblige. But if you want to hear a song from me, then I will give you one, but a song of defiance, a promise that I will never forget my homeland, and that there will one day be a reckoning for what you have done.

If I forget you, O Jerusalem,
let my right hand forget;
let my tongue cleave to the roof of my mouth
if I do not remember you,
if I do not raise Jerusalem
above my highest joy (vv. 5–6).

These two verses, at the centre of the psalm, are a personal statement, whereas the verses before and after are expressed in the plural ('how can *we* sing . . . ?' ' . . . all that you did to *us*'). Thus they stand alone, at the very centre of the psalm, with the structure of a self-contained song, even with a rhyme at the end of each line (*y'mini*; *ezkerechi*; *simchati*).

Though it is commonly understood as an affirmation of love for Jerusalem, one cannot ignore the violence of the curse the composer calls upon himself: 'If I forget Jerusalem, may my right hand forget . . . how to play my harp', the greatest curse a musician could wish upon himself. Similarly, 'may my tongue cleave to the roof of my mouth . . . so that I can never sing again'.

It is as if the composer had taken this little two-verse song, which may have had an independent existence as an oath of allegiance to the cause of restoring Jerusalem, and placed it within the wider framework of the whole psalm, to give it a context and added meaning.

The very day of Jerusalem's fall now becomes a rallying cry and warning to Israel's enemies: If the psalmist is to remember Jerusalem, then God has to remember those who destroyed it. (Though here the Edomites are cited whose precise role in taking advantage of the Babylonian destruction to harm Israel is not altogether clear).

Remember, O Eternal, against the children of Edom, the 'Day of Jerusalem' (137.7).

Against such a bitter background, the closing triumphant curse against Babylon is perfectly comprehensible.

The opening phrase (v.8) even contains a remarkable word play on the name of Jerusalem (*yerushalayim*) itself. 'Happy are those who repay you (*ashrey shey'shalem lach*) for all you did to us. Happy the one who grasps and smashes your babes against the rock.' May those who conquer you behave to you as you once did to us.

This is not the pious prayer of a later time of reconciliation, but the ferocious outburst of people in the midst of defeat, powerless-ness and despair. It is a song of partisans or others fighting for freedom. It is a contribution by a poet in exile from his land to the cause of those who wait and hope for return.

Its place in the Book of Psalms is something of a mystery. Other psalms express anger at enemies, but rarely in such a graphic way.

It does contain a prayer for God to act in defence of the divine city and sanctuary, and the Levite origins may have ensured its place in the psalter. Perhaps, in the end, it had to be included because it expressed so well a popular feeling, and may have been one of the sustaining forces in the people's hearts during the seventy years of exile.

This unknown singer was true to his oath far beyond anything he could have foreseen, for in later exiles as well neither his song nor Jerusalem has been forgotten, as a religious symbol but also in its full social and political reality.

2

Abraham

There are figures of such stature in the Hebrew Bible that it is impossible to deal with them briefly – and to do so leads to the risk of seriously misunderstanding their actions. So it is important to give more space to Abraham with whom the whole adventure of faith that is recorded in the Bible began.

We know nothing at all about the 'historical' Abraham. Archaeological materials may colour in something of the background of his life – but these details must be used with caution. The only witness that we have about him as a person is the Bible.

We do not even know precisely what the Bible itself intends to do when it brings us the story of Abraham or of the other patriarchs. The stories are cast as history, but there is no such thing as 'objective history' – for every historian is influenced consciously or unconsciously by many factors in the choice of materials to include. Why do we know almost nothing about the first seventy-five years of Abraham's life or the factors that led up to his call by God? To what social stratum did he belong? What was his relationship to the political powers of his day? Matters that today may interest us as social or cultural historians were considered unimportant for those who brought us the biblical narrative. Their interests were something else for they were writing what is perhaps best called 'prophetic history' – history that attempts to read the hand of God into human activities. They made their own selection of what they considered important from the legends, traditional stories and fragments of earlier records that were at hand. And they presented it in a way that is carefully written, shaped and edited so as best to serve their purposes. What we read, therefore, is not 'the true history of Abraham' but an interpretation of a figure who seemed significant for many reasons, but, above all, as the first person to try to mould his life so as to fulfill the will of the One God.

We do not know who the author or authors or composers or editors were. And even the clues that we sometimes think we have unearthed from the texts are ambiguous and possibly misleading. We do not know a great deal about their literary presuppositions or conventions or talents. They were clearly artists of a high order, but we assume that they were not conscious of art as a value in itself; for them, such gifts were subsumed to expressing as best they could the word of God. They wrote in a language of which we have only a small sample in the Hebrew Bible so that we do not know how wide its range of expression might have been. Many things that are puzzling or untranslatable, which we sometimes explain as due to the corruption of the text in its transmission, may merely be reflections of our ignorance of what lay behind them. That we can work so well with the Bible is both a tribute to the skills of those who composed its various parts and a great wonder.

I have stressed all this because I want to be very careful in what I say about Abraham, his faith and God. The only given we have before us is the Hebrew text. It is there that we must begin. Perhaps the best starting point is an examination of how the Abraham stories are organized.

Those who have studied the narratives about him will already know of one particular problem that has concerned Bible scholars. I refer specifically to some strange duplications of the stories. There are two tales about Abraham pretending to a foreign king that his wife is his sister. It is sometimes assumed that these are two versions of the same story that have been retained in different traditions. There are also two different stories about Hagar and her son Ishmael when she is forced to leave Abraham's tents and wander in the desert, there to be saved by an angel. These duplications and similar ones are puzzling, but it is worth examining where they actually occur within the cycle of Abraham stories.

In Genesis 12, Abraham receives his call, with the Hebrew words '*lech l'cha*', literally 'go for yourself'. We will examine the importance of these words later, but it is worth noting now that they are also found in chapter 22 of Genesis, the chapter that tells of the 'binding of Isaac'. The Rabbis already recognized the link between these two chapters, and they clearly form a sort of bracket around the cycle of narratives.

When Abraham arrives in the promised land, he finds a famine and is forced, therefore, to go down to Egypt. There he claims that his wife Sarai is his sister – the so-called 'wife-sister motif'. If, for the

moment, we ignore the fact that chapter 21 deals with Ishmael and
Hagar, we find that chapter 20, which precedes it, also tells of the
wife-sister theme, but this time when Abraham visits Abimelech,
king of Gerar. Thus, these two tales form an inner 'bracket' around
the rest of the stories.

In chapters 13 and 14 we read about Abraham's nephew, Lot,
how he separated from his uncle and went to live in the plain near
Sodom. When war erupts in the area among various kings, Lot is
kidnapped and saved by Abraham who meets the king of Sodom. If
we look at the equivalent place at the other end of the cycle of
stories, chapters 18 and 19, we also read about the rescue of Lot
from danger, this time with Abraham's bargaining to save the city of
Sodom and its subsequent destruction. So these two pairs of
chapters also match up in their themes and locations.

We are now closing in on the centre of the stories. Both chapters
15 and 17 deal with God's discussions with Abraham and the
establishment of the *brit*, the covenant, between them. It is made by
God's promise in chapter 15, and reciprocated by Abraham's
acceptance of circumcision, the sign of the covenant, in chapter 17.
The central chapter of the cycle, then, is 16, the story of Sarai's
barrenness, the taking of Hagar and the birth of Ishmael. The
importance of these events will be examined later.

Diagrammatically, we have the following:

Chapters

12a   The call.   '*Lech l'cha*'   Blessing promised.
  b   Abraham in Egypt.   Wife-Sister motif.
13⎤
  ⎬   Lot in Danger. Sodom.
14⎦
15   Covenant.
16   Hagar and Ishmael,
17   Covenant.
18⎤
  ⎬   Lot in danger. Sodom.
19⎦
20   Abraham in Gerar.   Wife-Sister motif.
21   Hagar and Ishmael.
22   The Call. '*Lech l'cha*'   Blessing confirmed.

The pattern of the chapters is concentric; that is to say, in
organizing and editing the materials a sequence has been built up so

that the first and last chapters match, as do the second and the penultimate, and so on. The sequence is: the call to do something extraordinary, then an episode where Abraham pretends that his wife is his sister, then something about Lot being in danger and the wicked city of Sodom, then the establishment of the covenant, and, at the centre, the issue of the child for Abraham, this time Ishmael. The order then reverses to conclude with a second call to go on a journey.

Whatever the origin of these individual chapters and their detailed contents, they have clearly been organized in a deliberate sequence to make a particular point or points.

When first calling Abraham, God says, '*lech l'cha*', go away from your land, your kinsfolk (or birthplace) and your father's house. A moment's thought will make us realize that these instructions are not a matter of geography[1] – you cannot leave your land without first leaving behind your kinsfolk and without leaving your father's house prior to that. The sequence has to do with increasingly harder emotional decisions – from your land, from the family in which you grew up, your culture and society, to the house of your father, the strongest, most emotional tie that a person has. All of these he is asked to give up to follow a mysterious God.

Yet this powerful demand is clearly matched in chapter 22 when Abraham is asked to sacrifice his son. The Rabbis saw this latter chapter not as the first, but as the tenth of a series of tests that God gave to Abraham, beginning with the leaving behind of his home. If we look carefully at the Hebrew, we find once again that the words '*lech l'cha*' are here.

> Take, please, your son, your only one whom you love, even Isaac, and '*lech l'cha*', go for yourself to the land of Moriah and offer him there as a sacrifice (22.2).

These opening words also build up slowly to an emotional climax with the naming of Isaac.

Both chapter 12 and chapter 22 begin in the same way, with similar emotional build-ups and the identical call to 'go'. The phrase '*lech l'cha*' occurs nowhere else in the Bible, and the Rabbinical tradition was clearly right when it linked these two calls and asked, with that remarkable simplicity and directness that can only come from an intimate knowledge of the text and its implications:

[1]An interpretation I first learned from Nechama Leibowitz.

Which was the hardest *lech l'cha*, the first or the last?

Initially, it seems that there can be no argument; surely, to sacrifice a living son was the greater, the most grotesque even, demand. Yet, what must it have meant for Abraham to give up his family, his country, his religion, everything that gave him identity, love and security, in order to go off on such a mad adventure? At the age of seventy-five he must have seemed as foolish and senile as Don Quixote. But to kill his son! Which was the greater *lech l'cha*, to sacrifice his past or to sacrifice his future?

Is God's demand purely arbitrary? If we read chapter 22 alone, as unfortunately too often we do, then, if we are honest, we must conclude that God is as mad as the Abraham who would obey such a God. It is worth noting, though it may not help much, that God's first word is not an imperative, but a request: '*kah-na*', 'please take'. Something is at stake for God, also, in this strange request. What is it all about?

There is one possible answer in the biblical background to the Abraham cycle. God has created the world and seen that it is very good (Gen. 1.31). Yet Adam, the peak and pride of God's creation, asserts his own will against God. Once cast out of Eden, a human being, in the form of Cain, becomes the first murderer, and from then on violence seems to be the characteristic of God's thoroughly disturbed creation. In regret, God decides to destroy the world through the flood, but preserves something through one man, Noah, chosen because he has the quality of righteousness (Gen. 6.8–9). It is God's hope that through this quality the world may yet be saved.

But it is not to be, for from Noah's descendants come those who build the Tower of Babel, when human beings again challenge heaven. So it seems that God attempts to refine the experiment still further. Now God will pick only one man (before that man has children) and test and refine him to see if he is the right material on which to base the new human society. Like Noah, Abraham, too, is righteous and God knows (or hopes) that he will hand on this quality to his children (Gen. 18.19). God will give to him and his descendants one small piece of territory, a part of the earth, a microcosm of the world, on which to create the model of the new humanity and society.

So he takes Abraham out of his land and offers him a new land. He takes him out of his family but promises that through him all the families of the earth will be blessed (Gen. 12.3). It is the most particularistic act on God's part to select just this one man, yet the purpose is to achieve the most universalistic hope, blessing for all humanity. What is at stake with the calling and testing of Abraham is no less than the survival and the future of human beings. How does God set about preparing Abraham for this task?

Two main themes are mentioned in God's initial promise which find their expression in the narrative before us. One is the land, the other – a large posterity. In fact, the two are obviously intertwined, for the fulfilment of the hopes about the land depend upon there being children to inherit it. God has promised Abram (as he is still called) that his seed will be as many as the dust of the earth (13.16) and, in the context of the first covenant (15.5), that they will be as numerous as the stars of the heavens. Yet Sarai, his wife, is barren and past child-bearing age. In this situation Abram's faith is clearly put to the test. Does he wait for a child from Sarai, which means going against all the logic of nature and reality, or does he do something himself to secure a child? In the event, it is Sarai herself who makes the suggestion that he take her handmaid, Hagar, as a wife so that Sarai may be 'built up' through her, perhaps adopt the child as her own.

Abram listened to the voice of Sarai (15.2).

When we pay careful attention to the Hebrew text we pick up certain phrases that have deeper implications than the conventional words seem to mean. Adam is punished by God because he 'listened to the voice' of his wife, Eve (Gen. 3.17). Rebeccah, when she encourages Jacob to steal the blessing of his brother Esau, twice tells him, 'listen to my voice' (Gen. 27.8, 13). As a punishment, measure for measure, she must finally send away her beloved son, Jacob, to save his life. What she does not realize when once again she tells him to 'listen to her voice' is that she will never see him again (Gen. 27.42).

In these Genesis narratives the phrase seems to be used in situations when someone listens to the voice, and obeys the voice, of someone other than God. It represents those key moments when the central problem of Genesis, the tension between God's plan for the world and the desire of human beings to control their own destiny, comes to the fore. Had Adam not listened to Eve, they would never have left Eden. Had Jacob not listened to Rebeccah he would never have suffered twenty years of exile; Isaac gave him Abraham's blessing anyway just before he left home (Gen. 28.3–4). And, in our case, Isaac would have been born anyway, without the complications raised by the birth of Ishmael. It is as if God's plan somehow always comes through, despite the detours caused by the actions of human beings. In our story the appearance of Ishmael is caused by Abram's listening to the voice of Sarai. It is she who will eventually ask Abraham to send away Hagar and the boy after Isaac's birth. When Abraham objects, God tells him that this time, too, he must 'listen to her voice' (Gen. 21.12) and let go of the son he loves.

What seems to be happening here is yet another test of Abraham's faith or trust in God. Will he wait for God's fulfilment of the promise or not? In the event, he takes Hagar and, indeed, the son is born, which gives us, in chapter 16, the middle point of our cycle of stories and the false climax. In the very next chapter, in the context of the confirming of the covenant through the rite of circumcision, God spells out what is intended for Sarai, 'I will bless her and also give you through her a son' (17.16). Abraham laughs in disbelief and pleads for Ishmael. God, however, is insistent:

> But Sarah your wife will bear you a son and you shall call his name Isaac, and I will establish My covenant with him as an eternal covenant to his seed after him (17.19).

Within this chapter both Abram and Sarai have been given new names by God, and these seem to confirm that a new beginning has been given to them after the false start with Ishmael. But why is it so important that Sarah, and not another wife of Abraham, be the mother of the future generations? Here we must speculate, but perhaps the two chapters on the wife-sister motif have something to tell us.

In the first one Abraham claims that his wife is his sister, and nothing more is explained about it. In chapter 20, when he is confronted by Abimelech, king of Gerar, Abraham gives some justification for his deception.

> But she really is my sister, the daughter of my father, but not the daughter of my mother (Gen. 20.12).

Sarah is both his wife and his sister.

Yet this sort of marriage is expressly condemned in Leviticus 18.19:

> The nakedness of your sister, the daughter of your father or the daughter of your mother, whether born in the household or born outside, you shall not uncover their nakedness.

It is clear that Abraham's marriage to Sarah goes against this strong taboo and, in normal circumstances, would be condemned.[2] Perhaps to reinforce this point, within the same cycle we have the story of Lot's incestuous relationship with his two daughters, producing Ammon and Moab who will become separate peoples, excluded from the Israelite family (Deut. 23.4–7). So again we must ask what was so important in the birth of a son to Sarah that it could go counter to what was later totally unacceptable in Israelite society?

Perhaps the answer lies in part in its very exceptional nature – the rule is broken in this case to show that the normal rule is the opposite. But deeper even than this must lie the working out of God's plan of selecting from this one man and his family the model for future humanity. God began with one individual, Adam, and took from his own body a part that was formed into the woman who would be his mate, so that with their union they could become again 'one flesh' (Gen. 2.24). Similarly, it seems that God insisted that the mother of Abraham's offspring should be as close to him in family ties as possible, even at the risk of breaking the incest taboos. Abraham and Sarah are 'one flesh', the new Adam and Eve.

The child Isaac is born, the promised heir of the blessing and the covenant. But what of Ishmael? In Genesis 21, he is sent away. As a son of Abraham he, too, must be blessed with offspring and a future as a ruler of mighty nations. It is interesting that Abraham is promised that twelve princes will descend from Ishmael (Gen. 17.20), equivalent to the twelve tribes that will descend from Jacob. But the centre of the stage belongs to Isaac. With him is fulfilled the promise of Abraham's initial call. After twenty-five years of waiting, after the false attempt to guarantee the promise and the future through Ishmael, at last it has all come true.

> Then (the Eternal) said: Take, please, your son, your only one, whom you love, even Isaac, and go for yourself to the land of Moriah and offer him there as a burnt offering upon one of the mountains of which I will tell you (Gen. 22.2).

[2]It is clear that Genesis 20 offers some justification for Abraham's behaviour – she really is his 'sister', so he has not lied. Nevertheless, the effect is to reinforce the incest theme. While the condemnation in Leviticus belongs to a quite different strand of biblical material, it represents what seems the normative view. The case of Amnon and Tamar in II Samuel 13.13 seems to be another exceptional case and, possibly, only a *de facto* solution.

In a moment, the whole promise and hope fall to the ground – this child, too, must be given back to God. Once before, Abraham had tried to guarantee the future through Hagar and Ishmael; now, even if God asks the impossible, is he prepared to leave everything in God's hands? The *Akedah*, the 'binding of Isaac', is not an arbitrary test, but the final stage in a refining process that begins and ends with the call of *lech l'cha*, to go on a journey for God.

The story is still savage and disturbing despite its happy ending. It is a given, a fact, an event that happened, a test that was passed. The angel who speaks to Abraham reports God's satisfaction with the outcome.

> By Myself have I sworn, says the Eternal, that because you did this thing and did not withold your son, your only one, that I will surely bless you and greatly increase your seed as the stars of the heavens and as the sand on the shore of the sea, and your seed will inherit the gate of its enemies, and in your seed will all the nations of the earth be blessed, because you listened to My voice (Gen. 22.18).

We hear at the very end that same phrase about 'listening to, obeying, the voice' which Sarai used when she suggested that Abram take Hagar. Now Abraham has finally listened to God's voice. The promises given at Abraham's first call are repeated and confirmed. Abraham has achieved everything. There remain only a few chapters which tell of Sarah's death and burial, the securing of a wife for Isaac, and Abraham's own death, as a sort of epilogue to the key events that have already been recounted.

Nevertheless, there remain some riddles about Abraham's behaviour that have to be addressed, which takes us back to his journey to Mount Moriah.

After three days' journey, Abraham lifts up his eyes and sees the place afar off (Gen. 22.4). He tells the young men who are with him to stay behind with the donkeys, while he and Isaac continue alone on foot. At the end of the story Abraham will rejoin them for the trip home. Who are these young men and what is their function in the story before us? They are not witnesses to the key event. They stay at the foot of the mountain while Abraham and Isaac make their own lonely journeys. It is as if they represent the world of daily life, a life that continues as normal, while this extraordinary act of faith takes place in private. As Abraham both literally and metaphorically rises higher to a peak of religious experience, on the borderline between ecstasy and madness, the rest of us can only stand back and watch in horror and wonder.

In the same way, only Moses can ascend the mountain to confront God at Sinai, speaking for the people, and conveying back to them the word of God. In such moments both Abraham and Moses are unique spiritual figures, going far beyond anything that we are expected to achieve. Never again in the Bible does God make the demand that someone sacrifice his child. Jephthah does so out of his own inner drive, and wherever else the wish to do so is expressed by the people, it is condemned as an abomination, as perverting the worship of God with practices that belong to the pagan cults round about. It is the great paradox of the Hebrew Bible that in such matters Abraham is *not* a model for the faithful, in fact, if anything, he is the anti-model. What he did once should never be repeated. Because he did it, Israel lives off the merit of his actions and is spared such testing again. Abraham is the witness to God's activities in the world, and we are the spectators to Abraham's actions.

We know nothing about Abraham's inner questioning and doubts. God says 'Go!' and we read that he goes – with no hint at the time lag between the command and the fulfilment. It is this seeming total obedience that is both the mark of Abraham and, in some ways, the most daunting thing about him. He is a flawed human being in other aspects of his life (for example, exploiting the beauty of his wife for his own profit in Egypt), yet, in this matter we are shown no flaw. So that yet again he becomes not really a model, but the exception – for even the prophets had their crises and questions about their vocation. He seems so sure and certain – and we are not at all sure and certain.

Then there is the great riddle. Why could Abraham question God about Sodom and Gomorrah and yet be silent about Isaac? His silence at that moment is enormously disturbing. We want his doubts, his anger, his despair – not this quiet submission.

It is the great power of Abraham that he knew when to raise his voice against God, to call God to account, to demand justice for the people of Sodom, the innocent and the guilty – to show his disinterested love for humanity and his deep concern for the honour and righteousness of God. Yet Abraham also knew the moment for silence, humility and submission to the will of God when his own personal possessiveness and pride were put to the test.

With such a figure as Abraham we can never be completely at ease. But without a figure of such challenging power and authority perhaps the rest of the Hebrew Bible would never have been created.

3

Loyalties

NAOMI

The Book of Ruth has two heroines, and the very structure of the book itself allows for an equal weight to be given to both. The first and last chapters belong to Naomi, the middle two focus more on Ruth. But to Naomi belongs the centre of the stage in the opening tragic account of her life and loss.

The movement of the story follows the gradual stripping away of all that she has – first her homeland, then the men who are part of her life. Now she, too, acts as if to complete the process and tries to send away her Moabite daughters-in-law. When they protest, she points to her empty womb that will never again be filled. She has no hope, no future. Orpah, her daughter-in-law, leaves, but Ruth stays.

We, the readers, can already anticipate here the beginning of the renewal to come, something that Naomi cannot see, locked as she is in her despair. At the end, she, too, will regain a child, born of Ruth, and her fullness will be miraculously restored, but now is her time for mourning.

And yet there are two points in that first chapter when something alters within her. The first concerns a tiny change of word order when she speaks. In 1.8, on her way to return to the land of Judah, she asks her daughters-in-law to leave with the words: '*lechna shovna*', 'Go! return! each woman to the home of her mother . . .' She gives her blessing and sends them away.

They weep together, but then the girls offer to return with her to her people. In Naomi's reply (v. 11) there is a slight change of language. She begins: '*shovna v'notai . . .*', 'Return my daughters! for I am too old to be with a man . . .'

She tells them to go as she has no more sons in her womb. Then

again she repeats her opening words (v. 12) '*shovna v'notai lechna*',
'Return, my daughters! go! for I am too old to be with a man . . .'

There are two slight changes here. The 'daughters-in-law' of
verse 8 are now addressed as her 'daughters'. And the words 'Go!
Return!' have been reversed to 'Return! Go!'

Perhaps these changes reflect a difference in her awareness after
their insistence on remaining with her. For at first her only wish was
to send them away: '*lechna, shovna*', 'Go (away from me)! Return
to your own homes!' What she wanted was for them to leave her to
her own private bitterness and sadness. Only with an extra effort,
almost as an afterthought, could she add the words that would send
them back to their own family homes. '*Go away* from me! . . .
Return to your homes!'

In a way she was herself adding to the process of loss, ridding
herself of the last reminders of her husband and children and
somehow both confirming and even increasing her emptiness and
loneliness. She was stripped of all human companionship in the
present, and her empty womb meant there was no hope of such
companionship in the future.

But the second time Naomi speaks, after the display of love
shown by Orpah and Ruth, she becomes again a mother, concerned
about the welfare of the daughters she loves – and the order of
words is reversed as she looks out for their best interest and not
merely her need to be alone: '*shovna v'notai lechna*', 'Return to
your homes, my daughters, go (to them) . . . there is no future with
me.'

Orpah leaves, Ruth stays, and Naomi returns to Bethlehem to be
met by the women of the town, wondering at her appearance. To
their questions she answers with words that are really a poem with a
very particular structure that it is important to recognize.

Do not call me Naomi (pleasantness)
            Call me Mara (bitterness)
for Shaddai has embittered me greatly.

                        I, with fullness, went away,
                        empty the Eternal brought me back.
Why do you call me Naomi
                when the Eternal has spoken against me,
when Shaddai has caused me harm?

The first three lines and the last three match each other in their structure. Both begin with the name of Naomi and end with the name Shaddai, a name of God that may be associated with either destructive power or fertility. The centre two lines of her lament sum up her whole story: 'I went away full, the Eternal brought me back empty.' But something more is happening with these words than just her statement of despair. For in the Hebrew the first word is the emphatic *ani*, 'I', but the last word, placed so that it must be read with equal emphasis, is 'the Eternal'.

ani *m'le-ah halachti*
y'reikam heshivani adonay

Something, again, has shaken her out of her dark prison, where she can only meet her own despairing reflection, to a response that comes from her religious strength – she returns empty, but it is the Eternal who brings her back. She starts her summary of her experience with 'I', herself, but ends with the actions and name of God.

The same change can be seen in the two outer sections of the poem which form a kind of sandwich around this statement. For in the centre of the first three lines comes her cry, 'call me Mara, bitter', but in the centre of the last three come the painful words, 'when the Eternal has spoken against me'. The precise intention of the Hebrew is difficult. Perhaps it means God has witnessed against me, and some would amend it to read 'afflicted me'. But again it is the Eternal who now becomes central to her thought, and with this a degree of detachment and distance from her suffering that is the first stage to the healing process. The very fact that she can cast her bitterness into a poetic form points to the move that she has made towards healing; the raw emotions have been transformed and refined. Perhaps now there is also anger, but at least she can speak of it, admit it to herself and even hurl it at God. She has begun the slow return to life.

I think the above is a fair reading of the first chapter of Ruth, and particularly the way in which Naomi is portrayed. But since there was in recent times a rather unseemly squabble in a scholarly journal about Naomi's character a couple of remarks may be in order. It is possible to read Naomi's character both sympathetically and unsympathetically. Her sending away of her daughters-in-law can be seen as the product of her desperation or as a selfless act to ensure that they have a new future with new husbands – or it can be seen as the action of a woman who is utterly self-centred. Both views can colour our reading of the rest of the book. Is Naomi looking to Ruth's best interests when she sends her to the threshing floor at night to meet Boaz, or is she really exploiting the young woman's apparent beauty for her own purposes? The text seems to stress the more generous view, but it is also possible to read out the opposite as well.

Part of the argument about Naomi's motives can be derived from one of the factors mentioned above – her apparent change of perception about Ruth and Orpah, from 'daughters-in-law' to 'daughters'. Because if you look more carefully at the text of verse 8, it is not Naomi who refers to them as 'daughters-in-law' when she speaks to them, but it is the author who informs us of this: Then Naomi said to her two daughters-in-law, 'Go . . . ' However, in verse 11 it is clearly Naomi who addresses them as 'daughters'.

So now we have another problem. Is the author merely acting here as a neutral figure informing us about whom Naomi is addressing, or is the author indicating to us how Naomi herself viewed the two women at this stage, and thus setting up the reader for the change of perception that comes after their loving response? Again the decision must be made by the reader, but it is important to note the genuine ambiguity present in the text.

It is also interesting to look at a couple of Rabbinic comments on this text and hence the way they viewed Naomi. The first one derives from a typical Rabbinic recognition of a 'problem' in the text. Verse 3 begins:

Elimelech died, the husband of Naomi, and she was left, she and her two sons.

Again the text seems straightforward until one notices a certain redundancy. We know already, from the previous verse, that Naomi is the wife of Elimelech, and hence that Elimelech is the husband of Naomi, so why repeat this piece of information?

There is a 'literary' solution to the question in that the sentence changes our orientation from the story of Elimelech, as the major actor in events so far, to Naomi upon whom the rest of the chapter will centre.

The Rabbis, seeing the redundancy, felt constrained to ask an entirely different sort of question. Elimelech had abandoned the land of Israel in a time of famine, something they considered a bad thing to do. (Abraham got into trouble for the same failure.) They even multiplied Elimelech's sin by suggesting that he was very wealthy and only left because he got tired of all his relatives and the local poor coming to him for support during the famine! All of this helped explain his early death as a punishment for abandoning his people. But, if Elimelech was punished, why wasn't Naomi as well? Answer, because she was not a free agent.

Elimelech died, who was the husband (and hence the one who controlled the actions) of Naomi.

She was blameless in this particular matter.

That is the Rabbis at their most legalistic – the comment being the second remark on this verse in Rashi's commentary. But to keep the balance right, Rashi's first comment, taken from the Talmud (*Sanhedrin* 22b), is an amazing insight that exactly matches the reading we have been making about Naomi's plight. The comment simply says:

eyn ish mate ela l'ishto,
'a man only really dies to his wife',

that is to say, the person who most experiences and suffers from the loss of a man is his wife. However much the children or others may feel, the wife is the one who has lived with him through the years of their marriage, and that relationship, however problematic at times, is the most deeply binding one. It is the widow who really suffers.

But lest we end on too sentimental a note, the Rabbis had another fascinating reading to offer of another oddity we have already noticed in the text. We noted how Naomi twice said to her daughters '*shovna*', 'Return!' – but in fact the identical word comes three times in her addresses to them (vv.8, 11 and 12). Heaven forfend that such a pious woman as Naomi would be merely uttering pleasantries at this crucial moment – rather she was expressing the teaching of the Torah. For what was the status of the two young women? Were they Jewish or not? (This is not exactly a biblical question; they seem to have adopted the religion of their husbands along with everything else.) However, for the Rabbis the issue of conversion was crucial, and the Book of Ruth was clearly an essential text to study for evidence of what the law should be in the matter.

So what was Naomi doing with her thrice repeated '*shovna*', 'Return!'? She was indicating that three times you should reject the prospective convert. Only if they persist beyond these three rejections, and thus show their sincerity, should you accept them (*Ruth Rabba* 2.16). Alongside all her other human qualities, we must also acknowledge Naomi as a teacher and source of Jewish law.

RUTH

The earliet readers of the Book of Ruth must have struggled with a potential prejudice against her – but it seems to have been the author's intention to highlight this issue. She is a Moabitess, and that conjures up in our minds the origins of Moab, the father of her people, born of the incest between Lot and one of his daughters (Gen. 19.32–38).

Even the law tells us 'a Moabite . . . shall not enter the community of the Eternal even to the tenth generation (Deut. 23.3). Worse still, during their wanderings in the wilderness, the Israelites were seduced by the daughters of Moab into going after other gods, which brought a deadly plague upon the people (Num. 25.1–9). So the frequent reminders throughout the Book of Ruth that she is a Moabitess reinforce our feelings against her.

Yet we also know her as Ruth, the daughter-in-law of Naomi, who remained faithfully by her side. The private woman Ruth seems far removed from the stereotype Moabitess. She bears the loss of her husband and is not put off by Naomi's attempt to reject her. Her sister-in-law departs, but Ruth stays. She identifies herself with the life and fate of her mother-in-law. Her words of loyalty have given her immortality:

Where you go, I go,
Where you stay, I stay,
Your people, my people,
Your God, my God,
Where you die, I die,
and there I shall be buried.

Perhaps within them there is some affirmation of her loyalty to Israel, even a formula of conversion, though we know of no such formal procedure in biblical times – we shall return to this issue later. However, what is clear is that the link to the people and its God is bound within the framework of a personal loyalty to Naomi alone.

It is her initiative that takes her to the fields the first time. The reason she gives is usually understood to mean:

> I will glean among the ears of corn of one in whose eyes I find favour (Ruth 2.2).

But this has long been seen as a problematic statement. As a widow and a stranger she is entitled by Israelite law to what is left in the corners of the field and to the gleanings (Lev. 19.9–10); also to any sheaf that is left behind and forgotten by the owner (Deut. 24.19). It is not, or should not be, a matter of someone's favour. So a recent interpretation[1] refers her statement back to the previous sentence that has introduced the name of Boaz as a relative of Naomi.

In that context her words would mean:

> I will glean among the ears of corn *so as to find favour in his eyes*.

The next verse tells of her success: not that she 'chanced upon' Boaz's field, as it is usually understood, but that she found his particular plot of land in the large open field at once, within the short time available for the harvest.

Why does Boaz notice her? We may speculate about her beauty which attracted his attention. In the middle ages, Abraham Ibn Ezra thought that she might have stood out from the crowd because she was wearing Moabite 'national costume'. But the text is actually quite explicit about how this came about. She is reported by the overseer as requesting to gather among the sheaves after the reapers (Ruth 2.7), which is not the usual practice. Since it is beyond the competence of the overseer to allow this he has to wait for Boaz to come to ask his guidance. Hence the remark about her standing nearby since morning (Ruth 2.7), not that she was simply hanging around, but she was standing there awaiting his arrival. By this reading there is calculation in her actions: she has deliberately brought herself to Boaz's attention.

---

[1] For this interpretation and some others in this section and the one on Boaz I am indebted to Jack M. Sasson's masterly *Ruth: A New translation with a Philological Commentary and a Formalist-Folklorist Interpretation*, The Johns Hopkins University Press 1979.

In the discussion that follows between Ruth and Boaz, she quite firmly advances her demands beyond his conventional politeness and generosity. In the end, as well as inviting her to his table, he actually accedes to her request to glean among the sheaves (2.15).

Ruth has little choice other than to take some sort of personal initiative. Given the nature of Israelite society, a woman alone had a hard time – hence the repeated call in biblical law to protect the 'stranger, the orphan and the widow'. In terms of their legal status and financial power, women were normally either someone's daughter or someone's wife. For both Ruth and Naomi survival was a major issue.

If Ruth sought to find favour with Boaz, it might equally have been someone else. And perhaps she was tempted. Boaz tells her quite distinctly to 'stay close to my young *women*' during the gleaning (Ruth 2.8). But when she reports back to Naomi about what happened, she records Boaz as telling her: 'stay close to my young *men*' (Ruth 2.21). Perhaps that is the reason this sentence introduces Ruth as 'the Moabitess' – reinforcing once again 'our' perception of Moabite girls as sexually attractive and active. But at this point Naomi firmly intervenes and instructs her:

It is good, my daughter, that you go out with his young *women* (Ruth 2.22).

And indeed Ruth does stay with the *women* (Ruth 2.23) to the end of the harvest. At the crucial moment of choice between her private emotions and needs and her responsibility, it was her loyalty to Naomi that won.

In the second encounter with Boaz, on the threshing floor, it is Naomi who has taken the initiative and sent her. That seduction of Boaz is intended seems likely – the secrecy, the perfumed oil. (Though the description of her washing, anointing and dressing (Ruth 3.3) remind us of wedding preparations (Ezek. 16.8–10)).

But behind the story of Ruth we hear another tale: how Tamar seduced Judah when she pretended to be a prostitute so as to get a child by him and thus safeguard her future (Gen. 38) – and indeed Tamar is explicitly mentioned at the end of the book (Ruth 4.12).

Sending Ruth to the threshing floor is Naomi's attempt to find a husband, home, security, 'rest' (3.1) for her. A calculated risk. But when Ruth speaks to Boaz, it is not only as a potential husband that she addresses him. For she speaks of him as a *goel*, 'redeemer', a term she has heard Naomi use of him after their first encounter

(2.20). This is a technical term for the member of the family responsible for getting others in the family out of debt and preserving the family land. Ruth speaks to him as the redeemer who can save not herself – but Naomi.

She has not quite got it right, which confirms the idea that she is acting here on her own initiative. There are others in the family with prior rights to redeem. But Boaz acknowledges that her thought for Naomi's well-being shows her deeper concern and quality. Each of the women acts altruistically on behalf of the other and each comes to succeed as well for herself.

At the end of the book, Ruth herself seems to disappear under the weight of dynastic considerations: her marriage is blessed with memories of the patriarchs and her child is a link in the chain to King David.

She emerges as a woman of compassion and loyalty, pulled by her sexuality and her pragmatism to find a rich suitor, yet yielding in the end to her duty to, and love for, her mother-in-law, her dead husband and the people and God under whose wings she has found her destiny. In some ways she is as much a religious pioneer as Abraham. He left behind his old life and world to discover a new faith; she left her world behind to enter the community that descended from Abraham. And the text of the book itself seems to make that analogy. Abraham's call is introduced by the words:

> Go, for yourself, from your land, the place of your birth and from the house of your father . . . (Gen. 12.1).

Boaz acknowledges how Ruth left 'your father and your mother and the land of your birth for a people you did not know before' (Ruth 2.11).

When the Rabbis discussed the Book of Ruth they asked why it was included in the biblical canon. It is expressed as follows by Rabbi Zeira:

> This scroll, there is nothing in it about impurity and purity, about things that are forbidden or permitted – so why was it written!? To teach you how great is the reward for performing deeds of faithful love (*Ruth Rabba* 2.15).

Though his question appears to be somewhat tongue-in-cheek at the expense of the overwhelming Rabbinic concern with legal issues, his own response cuts to the heart of the book. For it stresses the acts of *hesed*, 'faithful love', performed by Ruth (1.8; 3.10), her loyalty to the memory of her dead husband, the maintenance of his family name and land, and to Naomi.

But, as we saw in the case of Naomi, the book served as an important source of Jewish legal interpretation about the issue of conversion. The Rabbis were concerned to assure the sincerity of belief of someone who wished to convert, but they also debated about how much Jewish law they should know. When Boaz noticed Ruth they felt sure that such a serious and pious man could not have been attracted by her physical beauty alone! Rather it was her refined behaviour and the evidence she gave of her command of the laws of gleaning that made him notice her.

> All the other women used to bend over and glean, but this one sat upon the ground and gleaned. All the women would hitch up their skirts, but she kept hers lowered. All the other women would chat with the reapers, but this one kept modestly to herself. All the other women would glean among the sheaves, but this one restricted herself to gleaning among the ownerless corn. Moreover she would only pick two ears of corn that were found together and never three (as three was the smallest number that constituted a sheaf) (*Ruth Rabba* 4.9; *Yalkut Shimoni* ad loc.).

If she knew something of Jewish law, it was clearly because she had an excellent teacher in Naomi. How do we know this? From the Rabbinic interpretation of Ruth's statement of loyalty to Naomi. There are a couple of different versions of this, but the basic pattern is shown in this amalgamation:

Naomi: My daughter, it is not the way of daughters of Israel to go to gentile theatres or circuses.
Ruth: Where you go, I go.
Naomi: My daughter, it is not the custom of daughters of Israel to live in a house with no *mezuzah* (the little box on the doorpost containing biblical verses).
Ruth: Where you stay, I stay.
Naomi: We are commanded to keep six hundred and thirteen commandments.
Ruth: Your people, my people.
Naomi: We are not permitted to worship stars.
Ruth: Your God, my God.

Naomi: The Court has four kinds of death penalty, depending on the nature of the crime: stoning, burning, beheading and strangulation.

Ruth: Where you die, I die.

Naomi: The court decides in which of two sorts of tombs someone who receives capital punishment is buried (depending on the nature of the crime).

Ruth: And there I will be buried (*Ruth Rabba* 2.22 and *Yebamot* 47b).

Of course the list of instructions is built upon Ruth's words, and other versions do not specify the list of death penalties. But to Ruth's obvious generosity of spirit we should probably add a phenomenal memory and extraordinary commitment. Truly a woman of valour, but will Boaz prove to be a worthy mate?

BOAZ

Does Boaz, the third major figure of the Book of Ruth, have a sense of humour? He comes across as excessively solemn and patriarchal, always correct in his speech, pious in his greetings. We feel he is not young, though his age is never explicitly given. (Rabbinic tradition makes him eighty and recently widowed, hence available for Ruth.) He has power and presence. But what kind of person is he behind this facade?

When he first he meets Ruth he is very proper. He speaks to her as 'My daughter', the correct address of an 'elder' to any younger woman. He invites, or rather, summons her to remain in his section of the field and to stay with his young women as they glean. He has told his men not to molest her and she may drink when the water is drawn. He abides by the forms, the dutiful landowner.

Ruth's first response to him, 'Why have you been so kind as to acknowledge me when I am a foreigner?' (Ruth 2.10) seems to open up his reserve. For he admits he has heard of her, how she stayed with her mother-in-law and left her father and mother and birthplace to join a people she did not know before. As mentioned in the chapter on Ruth, we hear in his words an echo of the call of Abraham, who also left his father's house and place of birth (Gen. 12.1). Perhaps Boaz recognizes here the significance of what she has given up, beyond what would be expected, and the religious impulse that may be there. He invokes upon her the blessing of the Eternal, God of Israel, under whose wings she has taken shelter.

To Ruth's grateful response he extends further his hospitality – she may partake of the meal with the others, and perhaps in this way is more fully accepted into Boaz's family.

It is only after she has gone that the extent of her effect upon Boaz is shown. For he orders his overseer to allow her to glean among the sheaves, an exceptional act, as we noted in the previous chapter, quite beyond the requirements of the law.

And yet we still do not know if he is just being a generous host to a woman who has shown particular kindness to a member of his family, or if he has been personally affected by her.

At the end of the barley harvest, in the middle of the night, Ruth comes to visit him secretly at the threshing floor. Boaz wakes. In his startled 'Who are you?' he has dropped the formal 'my daughter'. But once Ruth has made her request he seems to slip yet again into his patriarchal role. Again she is 'my daughter', again he calls for God's blessing upon her for the loyalty she has shown in not going after the young men.

He seems to mean that by choosing Boaz, as redeemer of Naomi's family, she has shown concern about the redemption of Naomi's land, hence securing a future for her mother-in-law as well. She put family and clan loyalty ahead of her own private desires.

But then he spots a snag – there is another person who has the prior right to redeem the property of Naomi's dead husband and he must be given the chance. However, Boaz promises to sort the matter out. Then the ordered tones, the formal blessings, the logical policy, break down ever so slightly as he rounds off his promise with an oath, 'as the Eternal lives!' (Ruth 3.13). And a command: 'Lie here tonight!' The term is used elsewhere with sexual overtones (see, for example, Potiphar's wife's offer/order to Joseph – Gen. 39.7) as well as neutrally for merely sleeping. The Bible tells us no more about what happened.

The next day Boaz summons a group of elders in the gate, the 'lawcourt' of the city, and informs them that Naomi has sold the land of her late husband, and that the unnamed relative has the prior right to buy it back. The man, who would then get the advantage of the use of the field, is quite happy to redeem it. This comes as rather a shock to the reader, whose 'happy end' seems to have been snatched away.

Incidentally the 'unknown' redeemer is called in Hebrew 'Ploni Almoni', which is a sort of nonsense term, the biblical equivalent of 'John Smith' or 'John Doe', a name which serves both to indicate and preserve anonymity. We shall devote a somewhat less formal chapter to him later on.

Just as we have given up on Boaz, he somehow, with one sentence, manages to totally reverse the situation and send Ploni away utterly terrified that he might ruin his own family if he goes ahead with the purchase (4.6). How Boaz manages to achieve this depends on how we understand a particularly difficult Hebrew text.

Only now does Boaz reveal the secret of his readiness to marry Ruth. He explains (4.5):

> On the day you buy the field from Naomi (you should be aware) that *I* have acquired/married Ruth the Moabitess to raise up the name of the dead for his heritage.

Most translations explain this as if 'you, the redeemer, have married Ruth' and assume he would have problems with two wives, but the Hebrew allows for either Boaz or the relative to 'acquire' her. If Boaz marries Ruth with the express purpose of designating any children as 'preserving the name' of her deceased husband, and hence keeping the land within the family inheritance, there is a totally new situation. While Naomi and Ruth were childless, the new redeemer would have the land without cost. But if Naomi, via Ruth, got a new 'son' to inherit, the redeemer would have to support the widow and child and preserve the land for him. Since Naomi had no resources of her own, she would keep having to sell the land, and the redeemer redeem it, until the boy was of age – when he would inherit it anyway. The redeemer who thought he was getting a free gift, because of the secret marriage, was suddenly about to acquire an enormous financial burden.

So to Boaz he gave up his right. The man who refused to do his family duty and preserve the name of his dead relative passes out of history without even a name. He remains the anonymous Ploni Almoni, when he could have been remembered as the forefather of David and the Messiah.

But what does this closing episode reveal about Boaz? He set up the case so that the man would walk into the trap of his own greed, before pulling out the carpet from under him. He could have told of the marriage from the start, but chose the trick instead.

Perhaps he felt that the other redeemer deserved it, but that last glimpse of Boaz being perfectly proper and formal, but just a little bit sly, hints at a wry sense of humour beneath the surface of solemnity. He takes his leave with style.

Did something happen on the threshing floor between Ruth and Boaz? The biblical text can be read either way. Undoubtedly Boaz was tempted, which leads some of the Jewish commentators to examine his long sentence to her in the middle of the night. (Long sentences in such circumstances lend themselves to the suggestion that the speaker is trying to persuade, or control, himself or herself, just as much as they convey information to the reader. Joseph's long explanation to Potiphar's wife about why he couldn't possibly sleep with her is a case in point (Gen. 39.8–9). But the Rabbis also commented on the long rambling information given by the girls going to draw water from the well when asked for directions to find the prophet Samuel by the tall handsome young Saul (I Sam. 9.12–13)).

Rashi assumes that the proprieties were observed. He focusses on the first word that Boaz uses about staying overnight. The Hebrew verb *leenee*, has the neutral sense of 'staying overnight', without any obvious sexual connotation. In fact it is the identical word used before by Ruth when she told Naomi that 'where you stay, I stay'. In some sense, as elsewhere in the book, words expressing good intent or wishes come back to bless the person who uttered them. Hence Rashi:

Stay overnight – Without a man!

Actually he seems to be citing the midrash which elaborates a bit more:

Stay overnight – tonight you will stay without a man, but you will not have to spend another night alone without a man (*Ruth Rabba* ad loc.).

As for Boaz's oath, at this point Rashi becomes a bit more imaginative:

As the Eternal lives! – She said to him, 'With words you bring me out!' (Presumably Ruth's equivalent to a scornful, 'Promises! Promises!'). At once Boaz sprung up and swore to her that he was not just talking empty words.

But Rashi also brings a second opinion with the statement:

Some of our Rabbis explain that he was addressing (not Ruth) but his own evil impulse (often identified by the Rabbis as the sexual urge), which had begun to insinuate to him: 'You are single, and she is single, come to her!' So he swore he would not come to her except in wedlock!

So did anything happen? I would only add a broader dimension to the story, so as to confuse it slightly further. The pre-histories of both protagonists contain sexual scandals. Boaz is descended from the illicit union between Judah and Tamar (Gen. 38), and Ruth is descended from the illicit union between Lot and one of his daughters (Gen. 19.30–38). Somehow the tone of the entire Book of Ruth is one of hope and healing, of repairing the damage of the past and building a new future. Indeed it looks forward to the birth of King David. I suspect that part of the intention of the book is to 'replay' those scandalous events from David's ancestry, to have both protagonists acting in a more appropriate manner and thus 'repair' the past. The past cannot be removed, but it can be re-interpreted and worked through in a different way. That at least would have both Ruth and Boaz behaving like 'gentlemen' on that night on the threshing floor.

Perhaps it depends on which generation we belong to as to whether we see abstention on such an occasion as the most appropriate or the most inappropriate behaviour. Yesterday's scandal is often today's romance.

'ELIEZER'

His name has not come down to us. Jewish tradition refers to him as 'Eliezer' because an obscure reference is made by Abraham to one 'Damascus Eliezer' who might inherit his property if Abraham has no children of his own (Gen. 15.2). There is no direct proof of this identification, so he remains the anonymous faithful servant of his master.

In some ways he is a classical figure of folk-literature, the cunning servant, looking after the best interests of his master, though shrewd enough to protect himself from trouble. He is the forefather of Sancho Panza and Jeeves, the guardian of common sense and practical wisdom.

Abraham is old. It is time to set his house in order. Like his grandson Joseph will do on his deathbed (Gen. 47.29), he asks those who will survive him to make an oath to obey his last wish.

Do not take as a wife for my son one of the girls of the Canaanites among whom I dwell, but go to my land, to my birthplace, and take a wife for my son, for Isaac (Gen. 24.3–4).

The servant is cautious. It is a long journey; the family may agree to the marriage, but the girl herself may not be willing. Would Isaac then go to her?

He strikes a nerve. Abraham's journey was to reach his new homeland. His covenant with God included the promise of a son to inherit it. For his son to return to his birthplace now might betray the whole enterprise. And maybe he thought that Isaac was too weak to cope with the temptations of the land Abraham had left. Jacob, a generation later, could return to Abraham's birthplace. But it took him twenty years to earn, and then trick, his way back home. God would guide the servant to the right girl, and if not, the matter was still in God's hands to resolve as God saw fit.

The servant leaves for Aram Naharaim, with ten camels laden with Abraham's wealth. He arrives at the well where the maidens assemble, the important centre of village life where others (Jacob, Moses) will also find their brides. (In fact we so expect marriage partners to be found at wells in our biblical stories that when Saul meets some girls on their way to draw water, and spends some time with them, we almost anticipate such a result. The fact that nothing of the sort happens is a reflection of so much other 'unfinished business' in Saul's tragic life (I Sam. 11–13).)

The servant sets up a test so as to know which is the right girl. He asks God to act with *chesed*, with loyalty and love, to his master, for *chesed* is the love that seals a covenant, a love that is reliable and trustworthy.

Eternal, God of Abraham, let it come to pass for me this day, and act with *chesed* to my master Abraham: See I am standing here beside the well of water, and the daughters of the men of this city are coming out to draw water. Let it be that the maiden to whom I say, 'Please incline your water jar that I may drink' and who replies, 'Drink, and I will also give your camels to drink', she is the one You have given to your servant, Isaac, and in her I will know that You have done *chesed* with my master (Gen. 24.12–14).

The test is a challenge to God. It is also a real test. A thirsty camel can drink twenty-eight gallons of water, and there are ten of them![2] So Rebeccah goes to the well, lowers her pitcher, raises it, carries it to the trough and repeats the process over and over and over again. The servant watches in wonder, at the prompt response by God to his request, but also at the generosity, energy and sheer endurance of the girl.

When negotiations begin with her family, the servant is all subtlety. As has often been noted, he somewhat rewrites the history of his quest.

He begins by elaborating the enormous wealth with which God has blessed his master. But he carefully omits any reference to 'the Eternal, the God of heaven and the God of the earth' by whom he had made his oath (Gen. 24.3). This is not time to bring up potentially embarrassing religious differences.

Abraham had spoken of living *among* the Canaanites, but the servant has him dwelling '*in their land*' – perhaps implying that his master is not assimilated to those pagan peoples, merely residing there. And Abraham's more casual request to return to his country and birthplace to find a wife becomes more specifically 'go to my father's house' (24.38, compare vv. 3–4).

Throughout he emphasizes the miraculous nature of the meeting, the way that God had exactly fulfilled his request, how the very first girl who came out to draw water was Rebeccah. But this raises a slight problem about how he knew that Rebeccah belonged to Abraham's immediate family before he tested her! So he quickly readjusts the details of his encounter with her so as to make the choice seem specifically and solely aimed at Bethuel's family. For in actuality the servant had offered Rebeccah a ring and bracelets first and only then asked her name (vv. 22–23), but in his version of the story for the family the gift is given only after he knows she is the daughter of Bethuel (v. 47).

It is a brilliant piece of tact and diplomacy, appealing at once to family pride and religious faith, but also to family greed. It is garbed

[2] I am grateful, as with so many other biblical insights, to Nechama Leibowitz for raising the question of how much a camel can drink, and putting Rebeccah's test into a totally other perspective. Finding the answer was not so easy. Several phone calls to London Zoo taught me that there are camels and camels. I finally found the figure of twenty-eight gallons in an article somewhere, and subsequently lost it.

in a cloak of piety and miracle that seems part calculation, part sincere. No wonder they cannot refuse.

But why do these wiles and strategies of Abraham's servant deserve such attention? The chapter, with its detailed repetitions and variations, is one of the longest in the entire Bible.

It may be that the servant anticipates that Abraham may already be dead by the time he returns. When Rebeccah spots the figure of Isaac coming out to the field to meet the camel train, she asks who he is. The servant identifies him: 'He is my master' (24.65).

So two sets of loyalty are displayed in this chapter: the '*chesed*' of God to the covenant with Abraham, a loyalty that goes beyond the grave and that watches over the descendants of God's chosen one and friend. And the loyalty inspired by Abraham in his household. For the servant was free of the oath if the girl was unwilling to come. In fact, the whole fate of God's experiment, begun with Abraham, depended on the servant's willingness to find the wife for Abraham's heir. Had he chosen to act in any other way, without the bargaining skill and manipulation he employed, the result could have been very different.

Maybe he did have something at stake in the matter of Abraham's inheritance. If the task was as hard on Rebeccah as it would seem, perhaps he did want it to fail, and was astonished when God took him at his word and nevertheless pulled it off.

Once it became clear to him that this was indeed God's will, he accepted the challenge of the task – to convince this pagan family and the maiden herself of the value of this offer of marriage.

A proper reading of the chapter might make us feel those heart-stopping moments when God's entire plan could have fallen apart had the servant been disloyal or made one false diplomatic move.

God tested Abraham and helped him win a son. The servant tested God and Abraham gained a daughter.

SAUL'S SERVANT

Biblical prophets can make mistakes. This is not as scandalous a statement as it might seem at first. The Hebrew Bible knows false prophets – who were presumably professionally qualified but brought wrong answers from God. They were either scoundrels or, as Jeremiah's encounter with Hananiah (Jeremiah 28) might suggest, well-intentioned people whose judgment was clouded by patriotism or overwhelming political necessities. Prophets are human and prophets err.

But there is a story that suggests that even a 'true' prophet could be mistaken when his own private judgment intruded. It begins with one of those peculiar sentences that appear sometimes in the Bible. They look like an historical footnote, put in by an editor to explain something to a later generation of readers. This one occurs in the middle of the description of Saul's journey to find the missing donkeys of his father. When Saul is ready to give up, his servant suggests that there is a 'man of God' who might help (I Sam. 9.6). To Saul's objection that they have nothing to give him, the resourceful servant finds a little money.

At this point the story is interrupted by our 'footnote'.

Formerly in Israel, this is what a man would say when he went to enquire of God: 'Come, let us go to the seer', for what is today a 'prophet' was formerly called a 'seer' (v. 9).

Of course this raises questions about who the audience might be that would not know the term 'seer' (*roeh* from *ra'ah*, 'to see'). Perhaps more significantly the sentence draws our attention to this word that will be used to introduce the prophet Samuel.

The rest of the story is well known. Samuel anoints Saul and subsequently he becomes king. But his reign is troubled and he finds himself continually in conflict with Samuel. In part this is fuelled by Samuel's reluctance in the first place to appoint a king over Israel, in part by Saul's inadequacies. In the end there can only be one resolution. God intervenes to depose Saul having 'changed His mind' about appointing him (I Sam. 15.11). Samuel is sent on a secret mission to anoint Saul's successor from among the sons of Jesse.

Samuel, pretending he needs Jesse's sons to attend a sacrifice, for after all, what he is planning is treason, sees them assembled before him. When they arrived,

he saw Eliav and said: 'Surely before the Eternal is His anointed!' (16.6).

Then follows the famous rebuke from God when Eliav is rejected. We must assume from what is said that, like Saul, Eliav is also a tall and impressive figure. In fact we are forced to remember that Saul's stature, head and shoulders above his fellows, was one of the features emphasized from the beginning about him.

Bible Lives

A young man and good, and no man of the children of Israel was better than he, from his shoulders and upward taller than all the people (I Sam. 9.2).

Now, in a blunt rebuke, God says to Samuel:

Do not look at his appearance and the height of his stature for I have rejected him – for it is not how human beings see. For human beings see what appears to the eyes, but the Eternal sees to the heart (16.7).

Four times in this sentence comes the root '*ra'ah*, 'to see'. Samuel, the 'seer', is the one who cannot 'see' properly. In this matter he has not 'seen' to the heart but only to the outer appearance. It is Samuel's subjective judgment that has led him astray. He has admired the stature of the man before him and not waited for God's actual word.

The story unfolds as each of the sons of Jesse is rejected until finally the absent David is summoned. Is there irony in his description: 'with beautiful eyes and good to see' (v. 12)? Like Saul he is 'good', and again he is 'seen'.

In the printing of the traditional Hebrew text there is actually a break in the sentence at this point, so that we literally have to wait for Samuel's word. He pauses and hesitates and doubts and weighs, by now clearly uncertain in his judgment. And God must intervene impatiently to finish the incomplete business, as well as the second half of the sentence:

The Eternal said: 'Arise! Anoint him! For this is the one!' (v. 12).

Suppose we return to the anointing of Saul. Samuel was reluctant to give Israel a king on religious grounds, because the people wanted a king 'to be like all the other nations', and God alone was Israel's king. But behind that one can also feel Samuel's private tragedy.

As a young man in the sanctuary at Shiloh he had seen the corruption of the sons of Eli the Priest, and through his first encounter with God had learned that they would be killed. Now in his old age he had himself experienced a similar problem. His own sons, whom he had wished to appoint to succeed him as judges of the people, had been rejected by them because of their corruption. The desire for a king was also a rejection of Samuel's own deepest wishes for his family.

Because of this, was his judgment clouded in his choice of Saul in the first place?

The word had come to him from God that 'a man from the land of Benjamin would come to him' (9.16). The text continues:

> And Samuel *saw* Saul, and the Eternal answered him: 'Behold the man of whom I spoke to you' (9.17).

Unlike in the later case of David where God took the initiative, Samuel *saw* and proposed and the Eternal responded to *him*.

It now becomes clear that the sentence we noted at the beginning has a deeper purpose. Indeed it provides the reader with information about unusual vocabulary, 'seers' now being called 'prophets'. But beyond that it draws our attention quite specifically to the role of the prophet as the one who 'sees' and thus the potentiality for not 'seeing' in the right way.

Did Samuel 'see' only the outward appearance that time as well? Did he only assume that God had answered him because he saw in Saul something that satisfied his own ambiguity about the whole exercise – an inner weakness alongside the outer stature? Could God have made such a mistake about Saul that it would necessitate a 'change of mind' later, or are we meant to detect here a continuation of the questioning of Samuel's choice. Did Samuel speak for God or for himself at this crucial moment?

But if Samuel did get it wrong, what of God's instructions? Who was the 'man from the land of Benjamin' whom Samuel should have anointed?

There is another candidate. Alongside Saul was his servant. When Saul wished to give up, the young man suggested finding the 'seer'. When Saul objected that he would be unable to pay Samuel for his services, the servant immediately found the necessary money. This young man had imagination and resourcefulness, two valuable qualities in a leader. But he remains anonymous, literally hidden by the large shadow cast by Saul – an unknown youth who might just conceivably have become king.

4

Baddies

PHARAOH

Since 'Pharaoh' is the biblical title for the king of Egypt, there are many 'Pharaohs' in the Bible. Some can be clearly identified from external historical evidence; others, like the Pharaoh of the Exodus, are much harder to pin down.

So all that remains of this one, or rather 'those ones' – since one Pharaoh dies and is followed by an almost identical successor (Ex. 2.23) – is the biblical record.

The first one is described as a 'new king' (Ex. 1.8) and this has led to speculations that he was not the natural successor within the existing dynasty, but someone who took power by himself. Following this line of reasoning, the remark in the same sentence that 'he did not know Joseph' implies not ignorance, but rather a policy decision not to 'acknowledge' a group of people given authority and certain privileges by the previous régime (Gen. 47.11–12).

Joseph the first 'court Jew' became also the first Jewish 'middle man'. There is a cynical reading of the story of how he was taken from his prison cell to interpret Pharaoh's famous dreams about the seven 'fat' years to be followed by seven 'lean' years (Gen. 41.1–49). Joseph's interpretation was not so novel, runs the argument,[1] nor his solution to the problem of potential famine. Certainly there was nothing in it that Pharaoh's professional dream interpreters could not have worked out for themselves. But Joseph represented the ideal person to put the new policy into practice. Food was to be saved during the 'fat' years in Pharaoh's store cities, thus effectively

---

[1] I heard the outline of this interpretation from Rabbi Adin Steinsaltz in a study session in Jerusalem.

creating a state monopoly on essential foodstuffs. It was then to be made available to the people during the 'lean' years – but at a price. As the people found they could not pay anymore with 'silver' (Gen. 47.15–20) they had to sell their animals, then their lands and themselves to Pharaoh – the slave society was created.

Since such a situation would generate massive anger and resentment, someone was needed to be the figurehead behind this state appropriation of everything. Thus Joseph, for all the honour Pharaoh had given him, and for all his apparent wisdom as the great provider, actually ended up standing between the régime and the population, a highly dangerous and vulnerable situation. Like Jews in similar positions throughout history he was subject to manipulation and exploitation from above, and, when a scapegoat was needed, state-induced pogroms from below. In such a position of power without power, Joseph and his family were set up as the inevitable losers in any radical change of government, and the potential victims of a new régime trying to consolidate its hold.

It is the new Pharaoh of Moses' time who spells out what was to become a standard propaganda line throughout Jewish history, and one that has been used by demagogues everywhere against minorities.

> Behold the people, the descendants of Israel, are too many and powerful for us. Let us have a wise policy for dealing with them, in case they side with our enemies during a time of war and fight us . . . (Ex. 1.10).

That the Israelites were 'too many and powerful' for the Egyptians was patently absurd, unless one is deliberately working on the fears and prejudices of a population. And the threat of external enemies, as a rallying cry for shoring up an unpopular or shaky régime, is as old and as new as yesterday's newspaper.

Pharaoh's first moves have about them a classic simplicity. First, the applying of special taxes to the Israelites, requiring them to provide labour for certain national building projects (Ex. 1.11) – thus beginning the process of isolating them in the public imagination from the rest of the population and also physically wearing down their resources and resilience. The work they had to do was gradually made more menial, more difficult (v. 14), so that within a slave society, they became the slaves of the slaves.

The inner cohesiveness of the Israelite community was also attacked. Pharaoh appointed taskmasters, Egyptians, over the

Israelites, but set up under them 'foremen', 'officers', drawn from the Israelites themselves – a forerunner of the 'Kapos' of the Nazi concentration camps. These would gain special privileges provided they kept the work force to its quotas, and it was this enforced division of loyalty among the people themselves that the Pharaoh who negotiated with Moses exploited in his battle against him (Ex. 5.6–21).

All that is missing is the step, begun in secret by Pharaoh, of the systematic killing-off of the male population, something prevented at first by the midwives' refusal to obey orders. (See the chapter on Shiphrah and Puah.) But by then the status of the Israelites had been so reduced in popular consciousness, beyond the protection of the law, or else Pharaoh's régime, and his powers to enforce his authority, were now so strong, that he felt free to act quite explicitly (Ex. 1.22).

When Moses tried to intervene with Pharaoh, his response was to play the same trick that had succeeded so far. By increasing the burdens of the people, and accusing them of laziness, pointedly referring to Moses' request that they go into the desert to make a sacrifice (Ex. 5.8), he separated Moses and Aaron from the people they were trying to help.

And as slaves, with the responses of slaves, the defeated people turned against their would-be liberators with anger and the grotesquely absurd complaint:

> You have made us stink in the sight of Pharaoh and his servants, and put a sword into their hand with which to kill us! (Ex. 5.21).

There is about their remark a touch of gallows humour. Their children were being killed, they were being systematically worked to death, and this new intervention might give their oppressors an excuse to harm them! Pharaoh had won.

Of course, this was not the last word in the drama. Against the massive political, intellectual and technological power of Egypt, Moses brought the ten plagues. There are various degrees of progression through the ten as gradually Moses defeats the magicians of Egypt at their own game, until they, too, succumb to the plagues they cannot prevent.

The damage they do becomes progressively worse, climaxing in the death of the firstborn, matching the murder of the children. But beneath the surface, another political move is being made. For with each plague, Pharaoh is more and more separated from his ministers and his people – as each in turn accepts the true power of Moses' God (9.20–21; 10.7; 11.3,8).

In the end, only Pharaoh is left, stubborn in his isolation, acting against all reason, his own best interests and the very existence of his people. He leads his army in pursuit of the fleeing Israelites into the returning waters of the Sea of Reeds.

Pharaoh's plan for dealing with the children of Israel is clearly there to be seen in a careful reading of the text. An astonishing analysis which influenced the above is to be found in the commentary of Rabbi Moshe ben Nachman (Nachmanides, RaMBaN, 1194–1270) a Spanish Rabbi, mystic, philosopher, physician and Bible Commentator. His reading of Exodus 1.10, 'Come let us deal wisely with them . . . ', runs as follows:

> Pharaoh and his advisers felt it unwise to attack the people physically for this would be seen as a great betrayal, to attack, for no reason at all, a people who came to the land by order of the previous king. Moreover the people (of Egypt) would not allow the king to act in such a violent way for he had an agreement with them. Moreover the children of Israel were a great and powerful people and would put up a great war of resistance. So instead he intended to act with cunning so that Israel would not feel that they were being treated with enmity.
>
> So he required of them that they provide a levy (of workers), for it is reasonable to expect people who were not full citizens to provide a levy for the king, as indeed happened during the reign of King Solomon.
>
> Then afterwards he commanded the midwives in secret to kill the male children on the 'stones' in such a manner that even the mothers giving birth would not know. And after that he commanded all his people 'Any son that is born, cast into the Nile' (Ex. 1.22). His intention was such that he did not want to ask the army leaders to kill them with the king's sword, nor that they should be the ones to throw them in the river, rather he told the people: when any man finds a Hebrew child, let him throw it in the river, and if the father of the child cries out to the king or the head of the city, they can tell him to bring witnesses and then they would certainly see that justice was done!
>
> And when this permission of the king (to act violently on the children of Israel without incurring a penalty) became known, the

Egyptians would spy out the houses (of the Israelites) and enter them by night, concealing their identity, and bringing out the children (to kill them). That is why the text (2.3) goes on to say that they could no longer conceal the baby Moses.

Exodus is not a comfortable book.

GOLIATH

About the life of Goliath we know nothing. And it is just possible that we have made a mistake about the way he died.

The story in I Samuel 17 is so familiar that it hardly needs repeating. Goliath the Philistine from Gath went out daily to challenge the Israelite host: their champion against himself. No one dared to fight him until the young David, who had come to visit his brothers, appeared.

Ashamed at the cowardice of the Israelites, David himself took up the challenge. Refusing the armour of King Saul, the young hero went out to meet the enemy armed only with a sling and five pebbles taken from the brook. With his first shot he hit the giant in the forehead and sent him crashing to the ground. Then, taking the huge sword of the fallen warrior, he cut off his head.

So much for the version of the story we have known since childhood. There are some interesting side issues. For instance, because the Philistines controlled the metal-working industry, only King Saul and his son Jonathan were in possession of swords at the time (I Sam. 13.19–22), so that the killing of Goliath by his own sword had important socio-political implications.

But the story is known and loved as a symbol of the triumph of the weak against the strong, the innocent youthful hero against the experienced, powerful warrior, faith against the forces of destruction.

This already impressed the biblical writer who seems to give two different versions of how the giant actually died. In I Samuel 17.50 we read:

And David overcame the Philistine with a sling and stone, and he struck the Philistine and *killed* him – and there was no sword in the hand of David!

But the very next verse goes on:

And David ran and stood over the Philistine and took his sword and withdrew it from its sheath and killed him and cut off his head.

So does David kill him with the stone or with the sword?

The answer seems to be with Goliath's sword, as described in the second verse. But verse 50 interrupts the straight narrative as a triumphant exclamation of the writer to emphasize the dramatic turn of events – against all the odds he won, 'and there was no sword in the hand of David!' Despite the weaponlessness of David, and of Israel, with the help of God, the enemy was defeated – and only in the next verse do we get the details of how this happened.

And yet is that what actually happened? Or rather, since we are unable to recover the actual historical facts, is that what the text in the Bible tells us happened?

In broad outlines, the answer must be yes, but a recent study[2] has suggested that there are a couple of problems in the legendary version. For example, what happened to Goliath's helmet?

Most illustrations depicting the scene, from classical art to comic-book versions of the Bible, give Goliath's helmet a conveniently high front to allow David's pebble to get to his head. Unfortunately, such pictures as archaeology has revealed to us of Philistine helmets show a covering of the forehead, and some even have a part that comes down to protect the nose. So why would David aim at such an impenetrable spot – and anyway how did the stone reach Goliath's head?

In addition there is another long-recognized difficulty – for if the stone did hit Goliath on the forehead as he was advancing, how come, as the text explicitly states, that he fell on his face? Surely in such a case he would have fallen backwards?

The answer to both these problems lies in the Hebrew word *meitzach*, which is usually translated as 'forehead'. However, a word almost identical with it appears earlier in the same chapter in the description of the ponderous armour worn by Goliath:

> He had a bronze helmet on his head, and wore a breastplate weighing five thousand shekels. He had bronze greaves on his legs and a bronze javelin hung from his shoulders' (vv. 5–6). (The total weight could be anywhere between forty and sixty kilograms).

[2]Ariella Deem, '" . . . and the stone sank into his forehead." A note on I Samuel 17.49' *Vetus Testamentum*, Vol. 28,3 (1978), pp. 349–351. I am happy to acknowledge that I owe the closing thought of this piece to her splendid article.

The word we need to examine is 'greaves', the piece of armour for the shins, rather like cricket pads. The Hebrew term is *mitzchat*, and the similarity to *meitzach*, forehead, is evident. If we assume that the same word is indeed intended in both cases (and Hebrew grammar would allow this), and we pay attention to this long, detailed description of the enormously heavy armour that Goliath wore, then what actually happened when David slung his stone?

> He took from there a stone and slung it and struck the Philistine at the *meitzach* and the stone sank into his *meitzach* and he fell on his face to the ground (v. 49).

It has long puzzled the commentators how the stone could have 'sunk' into his forehead, how it could have acquired the force to penetrate the skull. (Excessive 'growth hormone' has been suggested to account for Goliath's great size and the softness of his bones.) But if the reference is instead to the 'greaves', then the stone hit the giant above the knee, it 'sank' down his leg behind the armour, necessarily open at the knee to allow the leg to bend, and lodged there.

When Goliath tried to straighten his leg, he could not and fell forwards, face down to the ground. In that position, helpless under the enormous weight of his armour, he was easy game for David to slay with his own sword.

Perhaps this helps explain the cryptic information given earlier in the chapter (I Sam. 17.38–39) that David tried on Saul's armour, but found it impossible to move in it freely. We usually read this as showing how small and frail David was compared to Saul and indeed Goliath, thus accentuating the scale of his victory. But the experience may have actually given him an idea about the flaw in this type of military attire. It was all right when you were up and marching, but once flat on the ground you were utterly helpless since you couldn't get up.

This reading actually reinforces the view that David went into the battle with a strategy, as well as his faith in God. Moreover, this model of how he used the weapons of the enemy against them became a regular part of his tactics.

It was David's skill that chose the target, and God's help that made him hit it. The stone brought the giant down, the sword actually killed him. Of course it is less dramatic, though more cunning, if David did not strike him in the forehead. But to the heel of Achilles, Jewish literature should now proudly add Goliath's knee!

KORACH

Israel rebelled against Moses' leadership in the wilderness (Num. 16–17). Among the groups and leaders representing different social, religious and political discontents, Korach is named as the overall leader.

> Korach, son of Yitzhar, son of K'hat, son of Levi, took (*vayikach* . . . and Dathan and Abiram, sons of Eliav, and On, son of Pelet, Reubenites. And they arose before Moses and also two hundred and fifty men of the children of Israel, leaders of the congregation, those called to the assembly, men of renown (Num. 16.1–2).

The text is curious. Korach is the subject of the verb 'took', but it has no object, so it hangs suspended in the air. Some translations amend it to read that Korach 'took' Dathan and Abiram and the other conspirators, or add the word 'men'. Others suggest that he took 'himself'. Yet the Hebrew text remains a puzzle.

No less surprising is the long list of ancestors attached to Korach's name – the Bible rarely goes back more than two generations. An explanation is offered by a family tree in Exodus 6.14–26.

It begins by tracing the opening family lines of Reuben, Simeon and Levi, the oldest children of Jacob. It then goes on to examine in

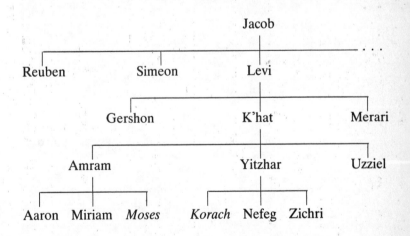

The Family Tree of Moses and Korach (Ex. 6.14–26).

greater detail the Levites, and particularly the family of Moses and Aaron.

Much of the extra information it contains makes sense only if we realize that this family tree is a sort of cast list of significant people for some of the stories to be told later, including Korach's rebellion. According to the list, Levi had three sons, and his second son, K'hat, had four.

The firstborn was Amram, the father of Aaron and Moses; the second was Yitzhar, the father of three sons, of whom the eldest was Korach. Korach and Moses were first cousins. Perhaps in this fact are sown the first seeds of rivalry.

The Levites have some reason to be upset with Moses and Aaron. In the centre of the camp was the Tabernacle. Serving it as priests, responsible for the entire ritual, were Aaron and his sons, and serving them were the Levites.

The descendants of each of Levi's three sons had different roles (Num. 3–4). The Gershonites were in charge of the tent of meeting, the tabernacle and all the major structures. The Merarites, descendants of Levi's youngest son, looked after the frames of the tabernacle, the pillars, bases and accessories, the least important parts. The Kohatites were responsible for the care of the holiest vessels – the ark, table, lampstand and altars.

But though it was their responsibility to transport them, they were not allowed to touch them directly. That was reserved for Aaron's sons, who would first cover them with cloth. Korach's branch of the Levites was tantalizingly close to the most sacred heart of the Israelite worship, and yet between them and the direct service of God stood the sons of Aaron.

Perhaps this lies behind the charge with which Korach and his rebels confront Moses and Aaron:

Enough of you! For all the congregation, all of them are holy, and the Eternal is in their midst, so why do you set yourselves up over the congregation of the Eternal? (Num. 16.3).

On the face of it, it is a plea for democracy, but beneath the surface is a suspicion that what is really at stake is the pride and status of Korach and the Levites.

Moses speaks to the Levites behind Korach, reminding them that they have a privileged status among the tribes in that they can serve God more than any others. Surely that should be enough for them?

This argument seems effective because nothing more is said of them.

Later, when he picks up this issue again, Moses speaks directly to Korach:

> You and all your congregation be before the Eternal, you and they and Aaron tomorrow. Let each man take his censer and put upon them the incense, and let each man bring his censer near the Eternal, two hundred and fifty censers; and you and Aaron each with his censer (16.16–17).

The two hundred and fifty men mentioned here are probably firstborn Israelites who had previously had the right to make the sacrifices until the Levites took over their role. In their desire to serve God in this way they had also joined in the rebellion. But Moses isolates Korach.

At first he speaks of 'you and your congregation . . . you and they and Aaron'. But at the end he concludes with 'you and Aaron, each with his censer'.

Korach has got to step out in front of the various groups, Levites and firstborn, he has been 'representing' and stand with Aaron alone before God. Each carries the censer for the incense, the symbol of the priest's role. When a fire descends from heaven, all those holding censers are consumed, and only Aaron survives.

At stake here is the power, and hence the danger, of the presence of God in the centre of the Israelite community. To approach this power requires a whole series of safeguards, of purifications.

Korach is caught between the desire to serve God and the pride of being the supreme religious authority. In accusing Moses and Aaron of 'setting themselves over the congregation', he may be betraying his own ambition. That is why he had to be stopped – to be that close to God, yet act out of impure, unrefined motives, could bring destruction on the entire community.

There is a short epilogue to the story. After the rebellion is over, the people still complain about it and a plague breaks out. Moses tells Aaron to 'take' the censer and intercede for the people.

> And Aaron *took* (*vayikach*) . . . as Moses had said and ran to the midst of the community (17.12).

Again, as at the beginning, the verb 'to take' is used without an object. What Korach wanted to 'take' was really the censer, the symbol of the priesthood, and to stand, like Aaron, the High Priest, 'between the dead and the living' (17.13).

DATHAN AND ABIRAM

Among the various groups that associated themselves with Korach in his rebellion against the leadership of Moses and Aaron (Num. 16), two men have the most prominent place – Dathan and Abiram, sons of Eliav, Benjaminites.

What underlies their revolt is open to a number of interpretations. As Reubenites, they would have had a considerable leadership role to play because of the power given to the firstborn family of Jacob. This power was clearly threatened by the radical changes brought about by Moses.

It has also been suggested that they represented the military faction, displeased at the recent disasters suffered by the people. The spies who had been sent to scout the Promised Land had returned with a bad report which led to internal divisions within the camp (Num. 14.1–10); an abortive attempt to invade had ended in disaster (Num. 14.40–45); and it was now made clear to them that they would have to wait forty years before they could again attempt to enter the land.

By this reading, when Dathan and Abiram stood defiantly before Moses at the entrance of their tents (Num. 16.27), it was not merely to make some further argument. They were *nitzavim*, 'taking a stand', which, in at least one other place, implies being ready to take military action (I Sam. 17.16).

It is for this reason that Moses took with him the 'elders', the civil leaders of the people, when he went to confront them – at stake was the issue of the civil or military government of the people of Israel at this crucial time.

The substance of their argument with Moses has a very familiar ring to it. Moses is attacked as the unsuccessful politician who is being accused of failing to live up to his pre-election manifesto.

The attack is made with a deliberate sarcasm. When Moses sends for them, their immediate answer is, 'We shall not go up!', presumably meaning that they refuse to accept anymore the authority of Moses as leader of the people, to come when he invites them.

They take Moses' own slogan about the land to which he has promised to bring them and throw it in his face:

Isn't it enough that you have taken us out of a land flowing with milk and honey to kill us in this desert? Will you also lord it over us!? You have certainly not brought us to a land flowing with milk and honey, to give us a heritage of fields and vineyards . . . Will you gouge out the eyes of those men?! We shall not go up! (Num. 16.13–14).

There is a Rabbinic view which consistently links the names of Dathan and Abiram with previous dissenting voices throughout the exodus experience. When the spies brought back a bad report and the people despaired, we read:

And they said, each man to his brother, 'Let us set up a leader and return to Egypt' (Num. 14.4).

Who were the two brothers who would have said such a thing? Dathan and Abiram!

Who were the two who went looking for manna on Shabbat because they had not obeyed Moses and gathered an extra supply the day before? (Ex. 16.11–27) Dathan and Abiram.

Who were the elders who criticized Moses after his first unsuccessful encounter with Pharaoh? (Ex. 5.20–21) Dathan and Abiram.

Who were the two Hebrews whom Moses had tried to stop fighting while he was still an Egyptian prince? (Ex. 2.13–14) Dathan and Abiram.

Incidentally, this consistent identification is nicely captured in de Mille's 'The Ten Commandments', with Edward G. Robinson making a villainous Dathan. Much research went into the making of the film, enough to be published as a book, and many Rabbinic *midrashim* (interpretations and legends) were included.

In all the above cases the Rabbis assumed it was the same two brothers making trouble and concluded: 'Whatever you can hang on this wicked pair, hang it!' (*Yalkut Shimeoni, Exodus* 167).

What is particularly interesting in this suggestion is the view that behind all these individual complaints and revolts is a consistent opposition to the leadership of Moses which found its climax in the Korach rebellion. We need to read these stories with a far more sharply attuned political eye.

There is one textual hint that does link up one of these episodes with the story before us. When Moses separated the two fighting Hebrews, one of them accused him:

mi sam'cha l'ish sar v'shofet alenu
Who appointed you as a prince and judge over us? (Ex. 5.14).

With one exception, the root *sarar*, 'to be a prince, "lord"', does not occur again between this Exodus passage and the accusation of Dathan and Abiram:

ki tistarer alenu gam histarer
Will you also 'lord' it over us, really 'lord' it!? (Num. 16.13).

That would explain why it is only at this point in the entire rebellion that Moses loses his temper (16.15) – for here he is attacked in terms that challenge his personal integrity as a leader, which ignore all that he had achieved until then, but, far worse, go back to that first moment when he gave up all the power he might have enjoyed as a prince in Egypt for a people that immediately betrayed him. Dathan and Abiram knew the exact weapon with which to hurt him the most.

Their fate has about it the ironic edge of much of the 'measure for measure' punishment in the Bible. Those who accused Moses of bringing them here to die in the wilderness will indeed die in the wilderness. Those who refused to '*go up*' to meet him will '*go down*', when the earth opens up and swallows them (Num. 16.30–33).

This solution to the rebellion seems drastic, requiring from God 'a new creation', a miraculous intervention into the normal working of the world. The reason seems to lie in the response of the rebels and their refusal to enter into a discussion. Moses presents his case and invites the people to choose – those who wish to dissociate themselves may step back. Until the last moment the door is left open for some sort of negotiation. But the Reubenites allowed for no such compromise, and Moses called for a violent resolution, placing the issue before God for an absolute decision.

Moses won, but the people remained unconvinced and continued to make trouble. A show of force seemed necessary, but, in the long term, solved nothing.

In Rabbinic thought, since the text says that they descended 'living' into the underworld, the rebels are still alive down there going round and round the world underground. One Rabbi reported in the Talmud that he had found a place in the desert where, through a break in the surface, you can hear them confessing: 'Moses was right and we were wrong!'

But from another point of view, Dathan and Abiram remain alive. Their defeat is not a triumph for the will of God but a tragic reminder of the failure of human beings to resolve their struggles for power.

5

Comic Turns

BALAAM BEN BE'OR

At the outset of their journey into the wilderness, the Israelites faced Pharaoh with the whole might of Egyptian military power behind him. At the end of their journey, on the brink of entering the Promised Land, they met another enemy quite as dangerous: Balaam ben Be'or, the sorcerer, a man with the power of the word.

In many ways we are too far removed from his world to understand the implications of this, yet Balak, king of Moab, felt it worthwhile to summon him from the distant Euphrates to come and curse Israel.

> For I know that whoever you bless is blessed, and whoever you curse is cursed (Num. 22.6).

We remember at once God's promise to Abraham at their first encounter (Gen. 12.3):

> I will bless those who bless you, and him who curses you will I curse.

Now this promise, too, is put to the test.

There is a theme running through the wilderness stories, a move from the concrete to the abstract. It is as if the further the Israelites move from Egypt, the land of magical manipulation and idolatry, the more they are to be weaned from all such things. They needed to see a staff turn into a snake to believe Moses at the outset. Now the word alone, like those they heard at Sinai, had to be enough. Perhaps in this way they learned to trust an invisible, intangible God who was nevertheless all-present and all-powerful. Balaam could manipulate words and hence the gods – how strong was their God against this most dangerous enemy.

Balak sends the elders of Moab and of Midian to Balaam to ask him to curse Israel (Num. 22.7). He invites them to stay overnight and promises to bring back the answer of the Eternal. However, the message he receives is quite precise:

You shall not go with them. You shall not curse the people, because they are blessed! (22.12).

Balaam is in a cleft stick. On the one hand, the word of God is pretty definite; on the other, he has his reputation to think of. In his reply to his visitors, he tries to hedge his bets:

Return to your land because the Eternal refuses to allow me to go with you (Num. 22.23).

What is missing from his statement is God's refusal of permission to curse Israel, for that would be admitting too much. But just as his report of God's words is edited by him to suit his own purposes, so is that of the messengers when they reach Balak:

Balaam refuses to come with us! (22.14).

For King Balak, who is obviously something of a businessman, there is only one possible interpretation of this report: Balaam is holding out for more money! So back goes the delegation, but this time it consists of 'princes' or 'ministers' greater and more noble than the first ones – he has upgraded the negotiating team.
Balak's offer has also improved:

Please let nothing prevent you from coming to me. For I will give you great honour and whatever you say to me I will do (22.16–17).

Balaam is caught and has to regain control of the situation. He could tell the truth and that would be the end of it, but perhaps greed or pride, or some animus of his own against Israel because of this embarrassment, now dictates his next move.

Even if Balak were to give me his whole house full of silver and gold, I could not go against the mouth of the Eternal, my God, whether for something small or great (22.18).

A pious statement indeed, though the princes must have

exchanged knowing looks at his mention of silver and gold – the fish is on the hook. Balaam invites them to stay the night while he finds out what more the Eternal will now tell him.

What happens next is a source of considerable confusion. God comes to Balaam in the night and says:

> 'If the men have come to call you, go with them, but only that which I tell you may you do.'
> Then Balaam got up in the morning, saddled his ass and went with the princes of Moab. But God's anger was roused because he went and an angel of the Eternal took his stand in the road as his adversary (22.20–22).

How do we explain this contradiction – that God tells him to go, then gets angry that he does so?

In the Middle Ages, Moses Maimonides, the greatest Jewish philosopher and legalist of his time, suggested a radical solution in his *Guide for the Perplexed*. He was quite prepared to read such non-rational events as this contradiction, and more particularly Balaam's talking ass, as prophetic visions or dreams. They did not happen in outer reality but in the inner experience of the prophet.

Something of the same conclusion was reached by Martin Buber and Franz Rosenzweig, who collaborated in translating the Hebrew Bible into German. They, however, based their interpretation on a very specific narrative technique that they recognized as operating in this text.

They noted that from the moment that Balaam tried to keep his options open by reporting only part of God's word to his visitors, the Hebrew word *yoseph*, 'to do something again', keeps recurring throughout the story. The men are forced 'again' to come back (v. 15); Balaam has 'again' to ask what God wishes (v. 19); Balaam has 'again' to hit his unco-operative ass (v. 25); and 'again' the angel stands in his way (v. 26). It is as if this use of a repeated word, a common ploy of biblical narratives, sets the whole episode from Balaam's first bit of trickiness in brackets.

Since God's word, once given, does not change, all that follows is a direct consequence of Balaam's attempt to manipulate that word for his own ends. The supernatural elements, the talking ass and the angel, fit into a sort of inner dream state in which Balaam now walks around. What he has heard from 'God', the permission to go with them, is what he wished to hear – but God's anger is the real response.

There is a second literary device that underscores this pattern. It hinges on the two different words for God regularly used in the Bible and which are interchanged throughout this chapter. *Elohim*, usually translated as 'God', is a general term for the divine and is used also in the Hebrew Bible for 'false gods', 'angels', and human judges. The special name of Israel's God, which we have translated throughout as 'the Eternal' is technically known as the 'tetragrammaton', the name made up of four Hebrew letters, *'yod'*, *'hey'*, *'vav'* and *'hey'*. It is sometimes transliterated in modern English versions as 'Yahweh'. From an early period Jews have not wished to pronounce this name, out of respect, and have substituted for it the word *adonay*, meaning 'Lord', the more conventional translation. It is often important in these narratives to see which name of God is being used and how they are interchanged.

Since Balaam is asked to curse Israel, he talks about speaking to Israel's God, 'the Eternal' (22.8, 13, 18, 19; 23.3). But in the night encounters he has with God it is *elohim* that speaks with him (22.9, 10, 12, 20, 22) telling him both to go and not to go! So the inner contradiction takes place within the conversation with the 'god' that Balaam himself conjures up. Just to preserve the distinction, between Balaam's 'inner god' and Israel's God that really controls Israel's fate, it is an 'angel of the *Eternal*', that stands in Balaam's way, is seen by the ass and eventually by Balaam (22.23, 24, 25, 26, 27, 31, 32, 34, 35). Similarly it is 'the *Eternal*' that opens the ass's mouth (v. 28) and finally opens Balaam's eyes (v. 31) so that he can see the 'angel of the Eternal' and recognize what has been happening to him. Thus the text very clearly distinguishes between the actions really performed by 'the Eternal', Israel's God, and the 'god' conjured up by Balaam.

Later, when Balaam understands what has been happening to him, he spells out the implications:

> God is not a man to tell lies, nor a human being to change His mind. Does God say something and not do it, speak and not bring it to pass? (23.19).

Balaam had the gift to be a channel for the word of God, but he wanted to use it for his own ambitions and purposes. The last threat on Israel's journey is reduced to a comical figure beating his loyal ass and, intoxicated by his own words, marching blindly ahead on to the sword blade of the angel of death.

BALAK

There are not many variety acts in the Bible, but occasionally a story is told that amounts to a comic turn. Balaam and Balak (in Num. 22–24) make a comedy duo, at least on one level, with Balak playing the pompous fool to Balaam's 'straight man'.

Their first long-distance debate as we have seen in the previous chapter, when Balak sends for Balaam to curse Israel, is an ironic exercise in non-communication. Balaam does not want to admit that he cannot do the job; Balak thinks that his excuses mean that he is holding out for more money. So the stage is set for further misunderstandings when the unlikely pair finally meet up.

Balaam puts on a good show as a sorcerer. He orders Balak to build seven altars and sacrifice seven bullocks and seven rams. With these preparations complete, he goes to consult the Eternal, who sends him back with a message for Balak. In proper prophetic style, Balaam begins his oracle.

> From Aram Balak brings me;
> the king of Moab from the mountains of the East:
> Come, curse me Jacob,
> and come, denounce Israel! (Num. 23.7).

Balak must have got very excited; this is just the stuff he's been waiting for. But Balaam suddenly changes course:

> How shall I curse whom God has not cursed
> and how shall I denounce whom the Eternal has not
>   denounced?
> For from the top of the rocks I see him,
> and from the hills I behold him.
> See! a people dwelling apart,
> not reckoned among the nations.
> Who can count the dust of Jacob,
> or number even a quarter of Israel? (23.8–10).

Balak is furious.

> What have you done to me? It was to curse my enemies that I brought you here; now you're heaping blessings on them! (v. 11).

Balaam, with a certain doggedness, reminds Balak of what he had already told him:

What the Eternal puts in my mouth, that is exactly what I have to say (v. 12).

Balak is not convinced, and clearly does not understand how to cope with poetry. He latches onto Balaam's remarks about the large numbers of Israel, and suggests he try to prophesy again, but this time that he stand where he can see only a few of them, then maybe he won't be overwhelmed.

Come with me, please, to another place where you can see them; but you will see only a part of them, not all of them, and curse them for me from there (23.13).

At this new location Balaam sets up another seven altars, performs another lot of sacrifices, and again goes off to get the word from the Eternal. To Balak's eager inquiry, Balaam breaks into poetry once more, but again with little comfort for Balak. He points out that God is not in the habit of changing His mind, and since He has commanded that Israel be blessed, Balaam cannot take it back. No one has seen wickedness in Israel; God is in their midst since the triumphant exodus from Egypt.

Having established this point, he becomes quite enthusiastic in his vision of Israel devouring their foes:

See a people that rises up like a lioness,
like a lion poised to spring;
not lying down till he has devoured his prey,
and drunk the blood of the slain (23.24).

Balak is perhaps getting an inkling by now that things are not likely to work out as he has hoped, hence his desperate:

Don't curse them and don't bless them! (23.25).

To which Balaam replies:

I told you so! Whatever God says, I have to do (23.26).

A lesser man than Balak might have given up at that point, but presumably he feels he can still salvage something from his investment. Again he picks up just a little hint in the oracle. Balaam has said, 'No one has seen wickedness in Israel' – very well, let's try looking at them from yet another angle. So off he takes Balaam to the top of a mountain, sets up yet another set of altars and sacrifices. But this time, since Balaam has also finally been convinced that the

Eternal wishes to bless Israel, he omits the usual hocus pocus, turns towards the desert, and the spirit of God comes upon him (24.2).

He has a vision of Israel like a garden planted by the Eternal, blooming, well-watered and flourishing. Again he sees great military success and conquest, with their enemies crushed and scattered. He concludes:

Blessed be those who bless you and cursed be those who curse you (24.9).

Balak is furious and claps his hands together. One can see his rage as he harangues the unfortunate Balaam:

It was to curse my enemies that I called you, and look! you've done nothing but bless them three times now! Get off back to your own place! I told you I would load you with honours – well, the Eternal has prevented you getting any honour at all! (24.10–12).

Balaam gains a certain dignity as he reminds Balak that he had already told the messengers that however much Balak offered, he could only do as God said. Ironically, when Balaam made this remark the first time, he meant it as a pious evasion of responsibility; now it has become horribly true. But having burnt his bridges, he sets about frightening the life out of Balak with a series of oracles about the fate of any number of local nations at the hands of Israel.

Balak seems to have learned his lesson from this. In a cryptic remark in the Book of Judges (11.25) we learn that in the end he did not attack Israel.

Balaam was less careful. Perhaps angered at the whole episode, he seems to have become associated with the Midianites and died among them in a war with Israel (Num. 31.8; Josh. 13.22).

But all that is yet to come. The king and the teller of oracles remain a perfectly mismatched comic couple: the pompous fool confused when his usual control over events falls apart, shouting in rage at his seemingly incompetent assistant: 'Here's another fine mess you've got me into!'

BALAAM'S ASS

Balaam is on his way to Balak, King of Moab, to curse Israel. God has refused him permission, but Balaam wishes to do it – so Balaam departs, and God sends an angel to stop him.

Two similar verses form a bracket around the famous episode of
the talking ass. In Numbers 22.20 God says:

> If the men have come to call you, rise up, go with them, but only
> the word I speak to you may you do.

At the end of the episode, the 'angel of the Eternal' says:

> Go with the men, but nothing but the word which I speak to you
> may you say (22.35).

Between these two, as we have already observed in the previous
chapter, Balaam has become a changed man.

> The ass saw the angel of the Eternal standing in the way, with its
> drawn sword in its hand, and the ass turned from the way and
> went into the field – so Balaam struck the ass to turn it back to the
> way. Then the angel of the Eternal stood in a lane between the
> vineyards with a fence on each side. The ass saw the angel of the
> Eternal and was squeezed against the wall. So she squeezed
> Balaam's leg against the wall and he struck her again. Again the
> angel of the Eternal passed ahead and stood in a narrow place so
> that there was no room either to the right or left. The ass saw the
> angel of the Eternal and sat down beneath Balaam. Then
> Balaam's anger blazed up and he hit the ass with the stick (Num.
> 22.23–27).

Balaam the sorcerer and visionary cannot see the angel standing
before him; his humble ass can. The ass takes evasive action. At
first, she can pass on either side, then only on one. Finally the way is
blocked. The further Balaam goes on his wrongheaded journey, the
further his options are reduced. He is heading into a cul-de-sac, with
death waiting at the end.

The three separate mishaps give him three chances. With the first
he becomes violent and another is hurt – surely that is the moment
to look at what he is doing. But the ass remains the external
scapegoat for a fault he cannot yet see within himself.

The second time the ass turns aside, Balaam too is hurt – surely
when he starts to harm himself he must see that something is amiss.
But again he beats the ass. The third time could mean his death had
the ass not sat down.

Balaam loses his temper. It is a typical biblical device that the
same phrase about his anger is used a few verses earlier about God's
anger with Balaam. Somewhere anger has to be expressed – for

Balaam must resent God's refusal of permission, and, of course, he cannot be angry with God.

That suppressed rage, first described as God's, now comes out where it belongs, but the direction in which it is aimed is still wrong. Now that the emotion is out, perhaps he can work out what is happening.

> The Eternal opened the mouth of the ass and she said to Balaam:
>> 'What have I done to you that you have hit me these three times?'
> And Balaam said to the ass:
>> 'You have acted contrarily with me! If only I had a sword in my hand, I'd kill you now!'
> The ass said to Balaam:
>> 'Am I not your ass that you have been riding all along till this day? Have I been in the habit of acting like this to you?'
> And he said:
>> 'No'.

Balaam does not seem particularly surprised by the talking of the ass. But she poses for him the question that should have been forming in his mind. Why is everything going wrong?

He still puts the blame outside himself – the ass is at fault. His threat to kill it with the sword adds some ironic touches: for the man who would destroy a nation with the power of his mouth cannot even harm an ass without a physical weapon – and even now he is blind to the sword of the angel that faces him. That an ass can talk should also remind him that the power of the word comes ultimately from God.

The ass could have explained about the angel, but merely reminds Balaam yet again that somehow his customary world is out of focus – can Balaam not finally see this? At last, with the single word 'No!', Balaam admits that something is wrong, and once he has been able to make that admission, his eyes are finally opened and he sees the angel that has always been there.

The angel explains what happened, but in a sense the information is superfluous. What Balaam has come to recognize intuitively has now to be worked through on a conscious level, but his perception has changed enough for him to be able to make that exploration and recognize where he has gone wrong.

So what is the ass? Is she, as the Rabbis thought, a miraculous beast created in the twilight period between the sixth and seventh days of creation? (*Pirkei Avot* 5.9).

Or is her speech, as we saw earlier in the opinion of Maimonides, merely part of a vision, common within the prophetic experience? (*Guide for the Perplexed* II, 42).

Did she really talk or were her braying sounds interpreted as words by a sensitive person?

Is this a biblical attempt at expressing an unconscious process through external events, resolving Balaam's inner conflict through the language of fairy-tale, legend or dream?

Is the ass a symbol of the human will, or the unconscious upon which our conscious mind rides; some deeper level of perception within us that gauges the direction we should be taking despite the distractions and diversions our ego makes us follow?

Perhaps, after all, she is only a faithful ass that one day saw an angel and saved her master's life.

The Rabbis had an interesting idea about the fate of the ass after this episode – it dropped dead! They gave a couple of possible reasons. The first is not very charitable. Since the episode was watched by the elders of Midian and Moab, they might have been so overwhelmed by the experience that they started to worship the ass. To avoid this God promptly killed the animal.

The other version is a fascinating reflection of Rabbinic sensitivity. They argued that from then on anyone seeing the ass would remember Balaam's folly and this would perpetuate his shame. Since, in their eyes, to shame someone in public was tantamount to killing them, it was better that the ass passed away instead.

MANOACH THE DANITE

When is an angel not an angel? Not a common problem, one might think. After all, are not angels all feathers and plumes, shimmering lights and haloes? Or, to be a little more rational about the whole business, if you have some sort of experience you identify as supernatural, it must have enough unusual features to make you look twice.

Not so, however, in the Bible – at least not always. Moses saw a bush burning, but not being consumed (Ex. 3.2), and Isaiah saw fiery creatures sitting beside the throne of God (Isa. 6.1–3).

But Abraham only saw three men visiting him to tell of Sarah's forthcoming pregnancy (Gen. 18.1–2); Jacob wrestled with what he took to be a 'man' (Gen. 32.25–33); Joshua saw a soldier (Josh. 5.13–15).

Even the word for 'angel', *mal'ach*, really means, in the first instance, a 'messenger' and is used commonly of a human being sent to deliver information.

So matter of fact is the encounter with angels in the Bible that, on occasion, a little reassurance is needed that the message actually comes from God. Moses suggests that the Children of Israel won't believe him unless he can produce a couple of little miracles to prove his claims – though perhaps he is still seeking reassurance for himself.

And in at least one instance, an important event in the saga of Israel's judges depends on convincing someone that the angel is who he says he is.

It is probably just as well that the three angels came first to Abraham with the good news. After all, Sarah laughed when she heard about it, and what might Abraham have said if his barren wife suddenly announced that, following a visit from three gentlemen, she was to have a baby?

In the case of Abraham, we can imagine a rather solemn and possibly dramatic turn of events. In the case of Manoach it all comes out as low comedy (Judg. 13).

The wife of Manoach, who is never named, is met by a person she recognizes as a 'man of God', a term used of prophets. He tells her that though she is barren, she will bear a son (Judg. 13.3).

She is instructed to avoid wine and strong drink and forbidden foods during her pregnancy, for the son will be a *nazir*, someone dedicated to God, whose hair is not cut and who also abstains from strong drink and certain foods (Num. 6.1–21).

She goes home to tell her husband, clearly overwhelmed by the experience, but perhaps also a little cautious, bearing in mind the implausibility of the story. So in her description, not only is he a 'man of God', but his appearance is like 'an angel of God, very terrible' (13.6)!

She repeats the angel's instructions, which seem quite clear, but Manoach entreats God for a further visit from this 'man of God', so as to spell out what to do with the lad.

And God heard the voice of Manoach, and the angel of God came again to the woman while she was sitting in the field, but Manoach, her husband, was not with her. So the woman hurried and ran and told her husband, and said to him: 'Behold the man has appeared to me who came to me the other day.' So Manoach rose up and went after his wife and came to the man and said to him: 'Are you the man who spoke to this woman?' He replied: 'I am' (13.9–11).

Manoach asks how the lad should conduct his life and what he should do. The angel tells Manoach to do precisely what he has told the woman. He concludes: 'All the things I commanded her, do!'

Manoach's next step is open to interpretation. Being a hospitable man, or possibly remembering what Abraham did in similar circumstances, he invites the angel to lunch. The angel apologizes that, even if he stays, he cannot eat Manoach's food, but if Manoach wishes to make a sacrifice to God he may do so. Manoach, still not knowing quite what he is dealing with, tries another ploy:

What is your name, so that when your words come true we can honour you? (13.17).

This may be a not-so-subtle way of establishing the possible paternity, or else he is following Jacob's approach in seeking the name of the man with whom he wrestled (Gen. 32.30). But he receives the same evasive reply that Jacob heard: 'Why do you ask my name?' and an enigmatic addition: 'It is wonderful!' And it proves to be a 'wonder' because when Manoach makes his sacrifice and the flame ascends from the altar, the angel of the Eternal goes up in the flame and is seen no more.

In panic, Manoach turns to his wife:

We'll die! because we've seen God! (13.22).

But with admirable common sense, she reassures him:

If the Eternal had meant to kill us, He would not have accepted a burnt- and cereal-offering at our hands, or shown us all these things or now told us all about this!

In due course their son, Samson, is born.

Manoach may never have recoved from the shock of the episode, or perhaps he was so overwhelmed by the destiny of his son, that he utterly spoiled him. Certainly, the young Samson seems to be very demanding when asking his father to get him a Philistine wife.

It might not even be too fanciful to see in Samson's repeated sexual involvement with strong women who betray him a reflection of the weakness of his father and a fulfilment of the betrayal his father feared most when the mysterious man first appeared on the scene.

Perhaps the dangerous exploits of his son drove Manoach to an early grave, for after only twenty years judging Israel, the martyred Samson was buried 'in the tomb of Manoach his father' (Judg. 16.31).

6

Esther

Esther, or at least the biblical book that bears her name, needs a special kind of treatment. Its complex interweaving of fantasy, wisdom and violence makes it more like a story out of the Arabian nights than something appropriate to a 'respectable' source like the Bible. But then the Bible would not be the Bible if it was only respectable. So scholars have debated Esther's historicity, and theologians have lamented its narrowness and violence and panicked at the absence of any mention in it whatsoever of God. And readers of all periods, especially Jews who treat it in a most disrespectful way in Synagogue during the Festival of Purim, have enjoyed it enormously. What other book has such a good villain as the wicked Haman, such a beautiful and resourceful heroine as Esther herself and such a comical figure as King Ahasuerus, with his endless parties, beauty parades and sleepless nights.

And yet beneath the razzle dazzle of the surface all sorts of things are going on, and Esther probably needs to be re-evaluated in each generation. At the turn of the century the liberal Jewish scholar Claude G. Montefiore, could judge the book as follows:

> The true reason why we cannot regard the book of Esther as divine or inspired are, first, because of the spirit of cruelty and of revenge, so that it is not too strong to say with Dr Adeney that 'its pages reek with blood'; and, secondly, because there is little compensation for this grave defect in any grandeur or beauty of teaching elsewhere.[1]

And yet a century later, after the experience of the *Shoah* (the

---

[1]Claude G. Montefiore, *The Bible for Home Reading*, Macmillan 1899, 1907, p. 405.

Holocaust), the murder of one third of the Jewish people, the Jewish theologian Emil Fackenheim can argue that this seemingly marginal book should now take centre stage of the Bible, precisely because it speaks to the modern human situation – a world where God is hardly apparent and chance alone seems to determine human fate.

Between such extreme evaluations of the worth of the book there is room for a lot of exploration.

One of the criticisms levelled by Montefiore has to do with the violence, and particularly the 'revenge' taken by the Jews on their enemies, once Haman's plans were defeated. Of this Montefiore writes:

> We can hardly dignify or extenuate the operations of the Jews by saying that they were done in self-defence. For we are told that all the officials helped the Jews, and that none durst withstand them. Moreover, the slain apparently included both women and children. There is no fighting, but just as there was to have been a massacre of unresisting Jews, so now there is a massacre of unresisting Gentiles.[2]

Since Montefiore read the book as a non-historical document, he recognized that this slaughter was 'a purely paper one' but that did not make it any the better.

Perhaps we should deal with this issue first. Haman's decree, which has never been as grimly close to reality as in this century, was sent throughout all the lands of the king. It commanded:

> to destroy, kill and utterly wipe out all the Jews, from young to old, babes and women, on one day, on the thirteenth day of the twelfth month, that is the month of Adar, and to take their property for spoil (Esther 3.13).

Robert Gordis has pointed out that biblical and ancient Near Eastern literature often used a technique of inserting a quotation into a sentence without formally indicating that this process was happening – it would have been evident to the reader. Thus, when the Jews were given permission by the king to defend themselves (Esther 8.11), some of the words of the original decree which is now being effectively countermanded, are actually included in the text of the new command. This is to indicate *what the Jews are to defend*

[2]*The Bible for Home Reading*, p. 403.

themselves from, but not to give them a licence to similarly treat their attackers.

> The king has given permission to the Jews in every city to gather together and defend their lives and to destroy, kill and utterly wipe out all the forces of any people or province who attack them 'their children and wives, to take their property for spoil'.

In the event only men are reported as being killed (9.1–6).

One feature that makes the book particularly complicated is the borrowing of material, both themes and actual wording, from other places in the Bible – particularly the story of Joseph in Egypt and the account of Samuel, Saul and Agag, King of the Amalekites (I Sam. 15).

It is possible to see the links with Joseph solely in terms of the fact that both are examples of the 'historical-wisdom tale'. Indeed this may have led the author of Esther to model his tale on that of Joseph as both show how wisdom precepts could be applied to practical life.

With regards Saul and Agag, the links are much more obvious. Saul failed to kill Agag the Amalekite king despite being commanded to do so by the prophet Samuel.[3] Haman in our story is an Agagite, presumably a descendant of the same Amalekite king, and Mordechai comes from the family of Kish, the father of Saul (2.5). So the two protagonists from that past encounter meet again in the Book of Esther. Only this time, not only is Haman despatched, but also his ten sons. However, unlike the narrative in Samuel, when Saul allowed his men to take all the spoil of the Amalekites for themselves, even though it was to have been dedicated to God, in Esther we are told three times most emphatically that no booty was taken when the Jews defeated their enemies (9.10, 15, 16). So the story in Esther is a kind of *tikkun*, or 'repair' of the past failure,[4] perhaps even written late in the history of the biblical period by a writer with some kind of messianic hope in mind – repairing the past in preparation of a new future.

---

[3]See the section on Ahimelech ben Ahitov for further details (below pp.96f.)

[4]See the discussion of a similar idea in the encounter between Ruth and Boaz on the threshing floor, which 'repairs' previous sexual encounters between Judah and Tamar and Lot and his daughters, in the concluding part of the section on Boaz (above p. 47).

Another approach to the book is to see it more fully in terms of Wisdom literature. Hence, as Shemaryahu Talmon points out:[5]

Esther and Mordecai contrast Haman not only in their role of true sages, but also in their capacities as representative of 'goodness'. Theirs is not the goodliness of absolute morality. Such a concept would not square with the type of wisdom exemplified in the story. Their virtues become apparent in the subjection of their private interests to the requirements of the communal weal, whereas Haman was prepared to sacrifice a nation in order to satisfy his personal hatred of one man. The 'evil Haman' (Esther 7.6) whose intentions are vile (7.4; 9.24) is opposed by Mordecai whom all his brothers welcome and who 'seeks good for his people' (10.3). The victory of Mordecai and Esther over Haman is a double score: the sage vanquishes the apparent wise, and the goodly-just the evildoer. It therefore constitutes a valid reason for the jubilation of the Jews in Susa and throughout the empire (8.15–17; 9.18–19); 'when the righteous prosper a city rejoices, and when the wicked perish there is cheer' (Prov. 11.10).

What are the characteristics that we must expect in a 'historical-wisdom tale'? Talmon describes the central struggle.

What is ultimately at stake is the position of one of the two (Haman or Mordecai) at court. The contest will be decided upon not by moral superiority or by divine grace, but rather by a ruthless application of all the ruses found in the book of the 'wise' courtier: 'For with cunning thou shalt make war; and in ample counsel there is victory' (Prov. 24.6). The more seasoned and better skilled will prevail. Success assures of the good-will of the king who judges by tangible results and not by motives. 'The king's favour is given to a wise (successful) servant, and his wrath to the malefactor' (Prov. 14.35). The court is a slippery arena in which to fight. The rules are set by the king: 'For the king's word hath power, and who may say unto him "what dost thou?"' (Eccles. 8.41), and vanquished and victor are decided upon by his whims: 'The king's wrath is as the roaring of a lion; but his favour is as dew upon the grass' (Prov. 18.12).[6]

---

[5]Shemaryahu Talmon, 'Wisdom in the Book of Esther', *Vetus Testamentum* Vol. 13 (1963), pp. 419–55, p. 448.
[6]'Wisdom in the Book of Esther', p. 433.

What Talmon does not do in his study is analyse in detail the stratagem of Mordecai, and for an insight into this I am grateful to a Shabbat discussion with the late Rabbi Dr König, *zichrono livracha* (may his memory be for a blessing) in Amsterdam some years ago.

The central problem focusses on the question posed in the Talmud as to the character of King Ahasuerus:

> *Melech pikeah hayah; v'had amar, melech tipesh*
> *hayah.*
>
> 'He was a shrewd king'; but others say, 'he was a
> foolish king' (*Megillah* 12a).

There seems to be much evidence to support the latter view – his extravagance, his wild rages in which he does things like sending Vashti, his wife, away, to his later regret; his apparent blindness to the actions of his advisers, allowing Haman to condemn an entire people.

On the other hand it might be argued that he is, after all, a survivor in a very precarious situation of court intrigues and attempted assassinations. When he invites Haman to lead Mordecai through the streets, is he merely the unwitting tool of God, or does he have his own ulterior motive?

If I may *précis* what I recall of Rabbi König's thesis, which in turn goes back to Rabbinic commentary, the *midrash*, Ahasuerus must be seen as at least a shrewd man. The dominating problem that he must face is survival, and that requires maintaining a balance between potential rivals to the throne, allowing each one to cancel out the other. The spectacular rise of Haman is something that carries dangerous implications for this balance – a motif frequently seen in wisdom literature. Mordecai, aware of this, seems to set about preparing himself to become the necessary counterbalancing figure.

It is, thus, not accidental that he discovers the plot to assassinate the king and makes sure that due warning is given (Esther 2.21–23). It is also possible that his refusal to bow before Haman (3.2–5), instead of having a religious basis, as is sometimes assumed, is instead a further ploy to establish himself as someone who does not kow-tow to the powerful vizier.

Perhaps this reading becomes clearest at the climactic moment when Esther invites the king and Haman to a banquet. It has sometimes been suggested that the double invitation (5.4, 8) is evidence of a duplication and points to two original stories that have been fused by the author. However, we have learnt to be more cautious about such duplications as they are commonly part of the narrative techniques of biblical authors – what matters is often the difference between the two versions. The first account establishes a framework, the second one develops or contrasts it.

In this case we may be able to recognize that both 'invitations' are essential. Here we must pay attention to the exact wording of Esther's two invitations which seem identical, at first glance, but contain one highly significant difference.

In 5.4 she says:

Yavo hamelech v'haman el hamishteh asher asiti lo.
'Let the king and Haman come to the banquet I have prepared for *him* (namely the king).'

But when she repeats the request that first evening at the banquet she says (5.8):

Yavo hamelech v'haman el hamishteh asher e'eseh lahem.
'Let the king and Haman come to the banquet I will prepare for *them*.

In that change from *lo* (him) to *lahem* (them), that change from a banquet for the king to which Haman is also invited, to a banquet for both of them equally, are focussed all the fears of the tyrant king. Not jealousy about Esther being in love with Haman, but, rather, fear of a coup – for when the queen starts showing an undue interest in the number-two man, it is time for the king to get worried.

And, thus, it is no coincidence that that night the king cannot sleep! (6.1). Nor is it surprising that he sends for the 'book of chronicles', the record of events that have happened in the kingdom. It is not because he needs a light read to send him to sleep, but because he is looking desperately for a rival to set up against Haman, someone, too, who has shown loyalty and the ability to discover dangerous plots against his life – and he finds Mordecai.

Furthermore, imagine his anxiety when, in the middle of the night, there, waiting in the courtyard, is none other than Haman himself. Is it not the time for the coup itself?

The *midrash* hits the nail on the head when it comments on Haman's answer to the king's question about what the king should do to a man whom he wishes to honour (6.6).

At the moment when Haman said: 'Let the royal apparel be brought which the king wears . . . and the horse upon which the king rides, and upon which a royal crown is set . . . ' (6.8) – just when he mentioned the 'royal crown', the king's face fell and he said: 'His time is here already!' (*Kohelet Rabbah on Ecclesiastes* 5.2).

Surely it is no coincidence that the king at once orders Haman to do just this – to *Mordecai*!, whom the king emphatically refers to as '*hayehudi*', 'the Jew', knowing full well that he is thus conferring honour on the enemy of Haman, whose entire race the Agagite had wished to exterminate.

It might be argued that this line of interpretation merely increases the secular underpinning of the book and thus makes it even more problematic as a religious work. Nevertheless, 'the best laid plans of mice and men . . . ' It still requires divine providence to allow all of the various strategems to work out, or not to work out, so that the Jews are saved. But by opening this political dimension, we are allowed to approach the book from a different perspective.

It paints for us not merely a fantasy world but the very real world of political intrigue, compromises and power struggles that are the background in which the drama of two thousand years of Jewish existence in the Diaspora has been played out. It is not a world of ethics or morality, but of relative ethics and the values of survival. In a world of capricious monarchs and tyrants, and there is clearly a bitter undercurrent to the book which should not be ignored, for all its surface charm, in such a world survival depends on divine providence, but also on precautions and subtlety and favour. It is a world where things are not judged by criteria of good or bad, but by the ethics of the seven-times repeated statement *im al hamelech tov*, 'if it is pleasing to the king!' (1.19; 3.9; 5.4,8; 7.3; 8.5; 9.13).

It is a world all too familiar to us as the stage on which Jewish lives were gambled for in the thirties and forties of this century, and in which statesmanship and a good secret service have to go hand in hand with piety and the ethics of 'the lesser of two evils'. Esther, in the jargon of today's spy stories, is a 'sleeper', someone placed secretly in a position of power until she is needed. To judge her behaviour in abstract moral terms is to misunderstand the choices that she has to make.

I have my own theory about the notorious second day of fighting that Esther requests. It is to extend the king's new law to the rest of the city of Shushan and not merely to the citadel, which suggests that there are enemies there who are still dangerous and that it is not merely a bloodthirsty whim.

But more significantly, dangerous to whom? For Esther's request comes not at her own initiative, but in response to what seems to be a leading question from the king (9.12).

Surely it is to his advantage that whatever members of Haman's faction that might still be plotting should also be put away, for, after all, it is Haman himself who has spoken of 'a certain people scattered abroad and dispersed among the peoples in all the provinces of the kingdom' (3.8).

It is interesting how careful a record the king has kept of events and of the number killed (9.11), and how it is the officials of the various countries who help the Jews. It reminds us that, however great Mordecai may seem to be at the moment, his power is there only because the king backs it. Moreover, it might be argued that Esther's decision to extend the fighting is as much a bowing to a political necessity forced upon her by the king as to any 'bloodthirstiness' that she shows.

The violence that she displays is only a reflection of the violence implicit in the system into which she has been cast. It is the violence of tyranny that corrupts everyone who is part of it. It is the violence of the unredeemed world ruled by human kings in which the invisible 'King above the Kings of Kings' is not readily to be found.

In such a world, the only way to assert other values is to insist that the festival, Purim, that is to be instituted to commemorate the event should take place, not on the day of the fighting itself, but when the fighting is over. It is the day after that is set aside for rejoicing; it is the deliverance that is celebrated, not the killing that had to accompany it (9.22).

I am not offering this interpretation as a way of exonerating Esther. The argument that one was only 'obeying orders' cannot be upheld. But what it does do is locate the source of violence outside of the will of Esther or Mordecai and in the nature of the regime, of their society itself. We are, thus, thrown into the heart of a real problem of contemporary ethics; the text *is* problematic, and it *does* raise difficult questions. But, for that reason alone, it should take its place alongside other Bible passages that either directly or indirectly raise questions about violence, power struggles or conquest.

Bible Lives

Let us take a second look at something which we have already observed and indicate another level on which our book functions. I refer to King Ahasuerus' worries about Haman, prompted by his mentioning 'the crown'. In contemporary parlance, Haman has made a Freudian slip, revealing what are his own secret motivations, ones that he has perhaps hardly dared admit yet to himself. He wants the crown, he wants to be the king – this king whose title is mentioned almost two hundred times in the book; this king around whom all the events revolve.

It is worth pausing a few moments to look at some other things in Haman's unconscious. We forget that the information that he is an Agagite tells us not only that he comes from the line of Israel's enemies, but also that he, too, is an outsider in the Persian court. When he speaks of a people scattered throughout the land whose laws are different from those of every other people (3.8), he is also describing, in a projection, some aspect of his own outsider status. And we can see the depth of his insecurity in the pathetic way he boasts to his wife and friends (who surely know it already) about his wealth, his many sons and his prestige at court (5.11) – only to add how all this means nothing to him whenever he sees Mordecai the Jew, the one man who has refused to acknowledge his power, the one man who, by his own existence, reminds him of his outsider status. For Haman, too, is insecure, part of a minority group, relying on his wealth or other keys to power to maintain his position, ready to invent a scapegoat to insure the continuance of his power. Haman is nothing more than the alternative face of Mordecai, a distorted reflection of the same character. The two are brothers under the skin. Perhaps it is that deeper relationship that Rava is pointing towards when he says in the Talmud that we are obliged to drink so much wine on Purim that we become incapable of knowing whether we are cursing Haman or blessing Mordecai (*Megillah* 7b).

There are innumerable other dimensions to the Book of Esther that could be analysed. If we are content to treat the *Megillah* (the Hebrew term for the 'scroll of Esther') as a funny book to be read once a year during the festival of Purim, then perhaps we are entitled to dismiss it. But if we are to treat it with the seriousness, imagination and care with which every book of the Bible should be approached, then it has much to teach and, more important, many profound and far-reaching questions to ask us.

7

Victims

PALTI BEN LAISH

Palti is a victim. He appears from nowhere, plays his two brief scenes, and disappears again. Events of great importance flow over and around him; he is caught up for a moment and then dropped as of no consequence to the grand scheme – yet he changes our view of the world.

Young David won the hand of Michal, daughter of King Saul, in the famous military exploit where he and his men killed two hundred Philistines and David brought their foreskins to Saul as the dowry. But Saul's subsequent jealousy led him to try to kill David.

Michal, David's new wife, warned him and saved his life by lowering him out of the window. She stuffed his bed so that it would appear he was still in it and stalled the men sent to find David by claiming he was ill. To Saul's angry inquiry the next day, she pretended that David had forced her to help (I Sam. 19.11–17).

There followed the tragic period of guerrilla warfare, with Saul repeatedly trying to trap and kill David. Despite brief moments of reconciliation, Saul's increasing irrationality made the estrangement even greater.

At one point (the exact time is unclear), Saul reneged on the marriage between his daughter and David. It is recorded almost as an aside in the context of mentioning David's marriages to Abigail and Ahinoam:

Saul gave Michal his daughter, David's wife, to Palti the son of Laish, who was of Gallim (I Sam. 25.44).

Nothing of Saul's motives is given. He was clearly concerned at the popular support shown to David for his military prowess. Worse still, David represented a threat to his own son Jonathan's succession, and Jonathan's friendship with, and support for, David must have made Saul's anxieties worse. But Saul's love/hate relationship with David is so powerful and self-destructive that it seems to have had much deeper emotional roots.

David's marriage to Saul's daughter meant another potential step towards his possible accession to the throne. The information that Saul has given Michal to another husband is strategically placed in the narrative between the two episodes where David has the chance to kill Saul and does not do so (I Sam. 24; 26). In the first David finds Saul in the cave, but instead of killing him he cuts off part of his cloak. Later he calls to Saul, shows him the cut robe and speaks of his loyalty in a moving attempt to persuade him that he wishes the king no harm. He speaks of Saul as, 'my father' (I Sam. 24.12) and Saul weeps and in turn speaks of David as 'my son' (v. 17).

In the second episode, David finds Saul asleep in his encampment and takes Saul's javelin and waterbottle, again to show that he had the king at his mercy and spared him. But this time, though Saul twice refers to David as 'my son' (I Sam. 26.21, 25), David no longer refers to him as 'my father', but only as 'the king'. From David's point of view the estrangement is complete.

Saul dies and David begins his rise to power. For a time, he is king of the southern part of the country. The north is ruled by Saul's surviving son, Ishbosheth (see also the story of Ritzpah), a puppet king controlled by his general, Abner.

When they quarrel, Abner decides to change loyalties and promises David to hand over to him control of the north. David agrees, but lays down one condition:

> Good, I will make a covenant with you. But one thing I require of you: you shall not see my face unless you first bring Michal, Saul's daughter, when you come to see my face (I Sam. 3.13).

Michal has been living under Ishbosheth's protection, and it may be that David is testing out Abner's power to deliver the northern kingdom as he has promised. But why David wants her is not entirely clear. Perhaps he still loves her – but there is little evidence of love in their later relationship and they will quarrel bitterly, each using the memory of the dead Saul as a weapon with which to score points against the other. More likely, therefore, is David's hopes that she will be a stepping-stone to his rule over both kingdoms, because, as the daughter of the former king, marriage with her would win him the loyalty of Saul's tribe and their allies. So Michal is herself again a victim of this power struggle between the old and the new king. Her anger with David and bitterness are understandable.

David sent messengers to Ishbosheth, presumably after Abner had prepared the way.

> Give me my wife Michal, whom I betrothed at the price of a hundred foreskins of the Philistines (II Sam. 3.14).

Despite the spasmodic civil war between the two kingdoms, either because of weakness, or so as to gain some temporary advantage, Ishbosheth agrees.

We meet Palti for the second and final time:

> And Ishbosheth sent and took her from her husband Paltiel, son of Laish. But her husband went with her, weeping after her all the way to Bahurim. Then Abner said to him, 'Go! Return!' and he returned (II Sam. 3.15–16).

It is just a couple of sentences in the midst of these great negotiations and rivalries of kings – but in those sentences is summed up the tragedy of one man caught up in events beyond his control, whose life and love is destroyed in a moment, and who has no power at all to change things – he is simply dispensable.

That one detail by the writer of the Books of Samuel alters entirely our view of the struggles and intrigues that go on around it. It shaves another layer off the glamour attached to David and reminds us of the human suffering beneath the surface of these great political manoeuvres.

It is one of those remarkable subversive moments when the Bible forces us to look at the dark side of the tales of our heroes, to ask what really matters and what price may legitimately be paid. Palti loses his fairy-tale princess, but for one brief moment he helps turn our perception of the world inside out.

URIAH THE HITTITE

We meet Uriah at third hand (II Sam. 11). He is spoken of, acted upon and, ultimately, disposed of, more or less off-stage. We see him only briefly, must guess at his appearance in these last few weeks of his life.

He is the victim of an old ploy of murder mysteries.

Question: Where is the best place to hide a corpse?

Answer: On a battlefield.

Kind David surely did not invent it, but he is one of the earliest to patent it.

Yet Uriah is not entirely a shadowy figure. Perhaps he is transparently simple. A loyal soldier, faithful to his trade and to his men, cast by unlucky chance as an inconvenience in the drama of the passion of a king – and thus dispensable. He died a soldier's death – almost. In the heat of the battle he was killed, or rather, abandoned to die.

The story is almost too well known. David becomes infatuated with the beautiful woman he sees bathing herself on her roof one evening. He summons her, ignoring the fact that she is married to one of his soldiers, sleeps with her and dismisses her, perhaps never expecting to hear of her again.

This is a new David. Established, secure, his energies unused, waiting at home in Jerusalem while his troops are elsewhere fighting for him. Throughout the chapter messengers run to and fro: about the palace with his amorous errands, to the battle front and back with his plots. Camelot has become Versailles.

Bathsheba sends word that she is pregnant. Perhaps the younger David could have faced the situation, taking his chances before the law. But for an older David, too much is at stake. Does he know that he faces the worst crisis in his life, one that will almost destroy him and embitter the rest of his days? He sends to Joab, his commander, to send Uriah the Hittite to Jerusalem.

Uriah has no paternal names. As a Hittite, one of the Canaanite nations long-since dispossessed, his position in David's army is unusual. He carries a Hebrew name, 'The Eternal is light', so possibly he or his father had accepted Israel's God. He was probably originally a mercenary who allied himself with David in the early days when he fled from Saul or at the start of his kingship. Uriah is included in the list of the 'heroes' who fought alongside David (II Sam. 23.39; I Chron. 11.41).

David facing Uriah is uneasy. He asks formal questions which become absurd: 'How is the "peace" (literally, *shalom*, "peace, welfare") of Joab, the general? How is the "peace" of the army? How is the "peace" of the war?' (II Sam. 11.7). The reader can hear him struggling through the small talk, trying to justify Uriah's visit for military purposes, waiting impatiently to pack him off home to his wife.

He sends after him a 'present', but the word '*masa'at*' also means 'burden' – with it goes the 'load' on David's mind (v. 8).

But Uriah does not go home, preferring to sleep with 'the servants of his lord' at the entrance to the king's house. 'They' told this to David the next day – who the 'they' are, how many, is unclear. Were these David's spies or was everyone in the palace observing this embarrassing affair?

David asks Uriah why he did not go home and Uriah, the faithful soldier, loyal to his troops replies:

> The ark and Israel and Judah are dwelling in booths (or in the place called Sukkot, the base camp) and my lord Joab and the servants of my lord are encamped in the field – shall I go to my house to eat, drink and sleep with my wife?! By your life and by the life of your soul, if I could do such a thing! (II Sam. 11.11).

Does he know? That is David's question no less than ours. Simple soldier or a man fighting for his honour in a very dangerous situation? David has merely asked why he did not go 'home', why has Uriah mentioned his wife at all? Perhaps it is an innocent remark, because sexual abstinence may have been a religious duty prior to battle (I Sam. 21.6).[1] Or was he turning the screw on the man whom he knew had betrayed him. And why take an oath on David's life and not on his own?

David keeps him a further two days, gets him thoroughly drunk, sends him home – but again Uriah does not go. A desperate David sends another message to Joab in the field.

> Put Uriah at the strongest part of the battle, retreat from him so that he be struck and die (v. 15).

The message goes back with Uriah himself – with monumental cynicism David exploits that soldierly loyalty to the end. Joab obeys. Uriah dies.

There is just the possibility that all is not quite as simple as it seems. Uriah refers to 'the servants of his lord', but who is his 'lord'? It should be David, but clearly he speaks instead of Joab as his 'lord' (v. 11)? Is there a hint here of divided loyalties? The throne is still not secure. Joab who plays the part of 'king-maker' on a number of occasions and kills off his own military rivals, is the next most

[1]This was an argument used by David – see section on Ahimelech ben Ahitov (below p. 97).

powerful man in the country. David even warns Solomon on his deathbed to dispose of him. If Uriah is one of Joab's supporters, that would explain why Joab makes sure that some of David's men are also killed in that same battle (v. 17). So perhaps on a purely political level some question of potential treason may lie beneath the surface of David's violent act.

But that does not excuse or justify it, nor does David ever escape the consequences, nor deny his responsibility when confronted with the truth. Uriah the Hittite dies a hero's death, at least on the surface, but carries with him to the grave the secret neither David nor the reader can ever discover: How much did he know?

BATHSHEBA BAT ELIAM

Bathsheba is as enigmatic as she is beautiful. She is a creature of sexual fantasy, temptress or simple innocent. A dream figure of the night – alone, naked, bathing on the roof, unaware she is overlooked, vulnerable at her most intimate moments. Seen, desired, summoned, yielding and dismissed. Never to trouble the dreamer again, lying on his couch on a warm, scented summer night in the palace of the king.

But Bathsheba was real, as was her pregnancy, and David's fantasy had its tragic consequences. Yet what of her own feelings? Who was she as a person?

She was a married woman in a patriarchal society. Israelite culture could tolerate almost any crime against property, but was shaken to the core of its self-esteem by an assault upon the family, with its underlying threat to male potency and authority. Adultery meant death. Was she even more frightened of the will of the king? Or flattered at his attentions? Perhaps ambitious at the thought of future benefits, even scheming, making herself visible and available? Or merely simple, naive? And what of her marriage to Uriah the Hittite, the soldier who preferred to stay loyally with his troops rather than return to the arms of his wife? Was his death a relief or a tragedy to the young widow, bewildered, compromised and fearful?

Nothing in the episode of her first encounter with David (II Sam. 11) can even begin to answer these questions. Like the fantasy she is in this tale, we can weave around her whatever details or explanations we wish. She can be victim or mistress of her own fate, a blank screen on which to project our innuendo or desire.

It is to an older Bathsheba we must turn for a clue. That first child born of the illicit affair dies. But the second one, born after her marriage to David, lives, is named by him Solomon, *shlomo*, 'peace', perhaps in the hope of a newly-won peace, and called, at God's word, Yedidiah, 'beloved of the Eternal'.

Years have passed. David has witnessed the death of two of his sons, has seen his crime with Bathsheba and Uriah reproduced in distorted ways in his own children. Now weak and dying, the succession to the throne is unresolved.

Adonijah, handsome, headstrong, the image of a young David, stakes his claim, carrying with him Joab, commander of the army, and Aviathar, David's priest.[2] But there is another faction, also in part military, but including Nathan the prophet, who cannot accept this choice. Nathan, who had rebuked David after the Bathsheba affair, but had also brought the message of forgiveness from God and the name Yedidiah, chooses Solomon.

It is he who approaches Bathsheba to take action. He offers advice, pointing out that she and Solomon are at risk if Adonijah succeeds. She should go to David, remind him that he promised the throne to Solomon. Nathan will then come in at the appropriate time and reinforce her words (I Kings 1.11–14). There is no former mention of such a promise from David. Has Bathsheba been unaware of the dangers she faces? Or merely helpless in the situation?

She follows Nathan's advice, but her closing words to David have a nuance that only she could dredge out of the past of their shared guilt and shared suffering.

And you, my lord, the king, the eyes of all Israel are upon you to tell them who should sit upon the throne of my lord, the king after him. But it could be that when my lord, the king sleeps with his ancestors, then I and my son Solomon will be '*hataim*' (I Kings 1.20–21).

The word *hataim* has its origins in the idea of 'missing the mark', 'failing to hit the target'. Perhaps it means here, 'lost', 'failures', 'losers', losing their rank or even doomed to die. But its derived sense means a deeper religious failure, to 'sin'. In that sense it is the word David used of himself when Nathan revealed the depth of his crimes against Uriah:

[2]See the story of Ahimelech ben Ahitov (below p. 99).

I have sinned (*hatati*) against the Eternal! (II Sam. 12.13).

Now Bathsheba says the word – I and my son Solomon will still be trapped in that sin and condemned by it if you do not act. For a moment she steps out of her role of a woman manipulated by strong men for their own purposes. She is now the one who acts.

The ploy succeeds, but Bathsheba has one more part to play.

An aging David had been kept warm in bed by a new young concubine, Abishag. David is dead, Solomon enthroned. Now Adonijah comes cautiously to Bathsheba with a request.

You know I should have had the kingdom and all Israel turned to me to rule, but the kingdom went otherwise and became my brother's, which was the Eternal's doing. Now I have a request of you – do not refuse me. Please speak to King Solomon, for he will not refuse you, that he give me Abishag the Shunammite as a wife (I Kings 2.15–17).

Bathsheba agreed.

Was she naive, perhaps wishing to make up to Adonijah with this small request for the loss of the kingdom? Or sentimental about someone else's love affair? Solomon at once saw the political implications of Adonijah's request. To marry the former king's concubine would symbolically strengthen his claim on the throne.[3] At Solomon's command Adonijah was killed.

Did Bathsheba agree to Adonijah's request because she guessed the consequences, once again fighting for Solomon's future? Years of court intrigue may have filled out the dimensions of the young girl who once gave herself to the king. From creature of fantasy to aging Queen Mother, she retains her mystery, if not her allure, a survivor in a violent world.

AHIMELECH BEN AHITOV

One imagines an old man, grey-haired, bearded, dressed in the simple clothing of a priest, his garments no longer white in the dusty courtyard of the sanctuary, perhaps spotted with the blood of the daily sacrifices. For Nob would have been a busy centre for pilgrimage and worship.

[3]See the story of Ritzpah (above p. 9) for other examples.

Or maybe he was younger, newly elevated to the office. What, after all, did it take to become priest at an important shrine like Nob? Piety or politics, or a subtle blend of the two? Was he naive to have been deceived by David or merely lacking sufficient caution. No one in high office could afford to be entirely without guile, or at least aware of personalities and political currents, with Saul on the throne of Israel.

David, in flight from King Saul, comes to Nob, to Ahimelech ben Ahitov, the priest. The latter trembles on seeing him and comes to meet him with a question. Does he know of Saul's displeasure, or is he merely a man of peace, worried at the presence of a famous warrior at his sanctuary? He is surprised to see David unaccompanied.

Why are you alone, and no one with you? (I Sam. 21.2).

David has a ready answer:

The king gave me an order and said: 'Let no one know anything of the matter on which I send you and about which I have commanded you.' As for my men, I have directed them to a secret place. Now what do you have to hand? Let me have five loaves of bread or whatever is here (I Sam. 21.3–4).

Is Ahimelech flattered to be part of his secret mission, perhaps setting aside his fears too soon? He moves on to practical matters. The only bread available is dedicated to God and set aside for ritual purposes. Have David's men kept themselves from women, for an emission would make them ritually unclean?

David's answer, slightly ambiguous, seems suitably pious.

Women have been kept from us for the past few days since I set out. The equipment of the men is holy even when it is a common journey, how much more today when the equipment is to be sanctified (v. 6).

So Ahimelech gives him the sanctified bread. Having gone so far David carries his bluff further, even though it goes beyond common sense.

Do you not have here to hand a spear or sword, for I was unable to take my own sword or weapons, for the word of the king was very urgent? (v. 9).

Perhaps Ahimelech is truly simple, or else moved by the seeming rightness of the matter. For stored in this sacred place is the sword of Goliath, presumably dedicated to God in thanksgiving for David's victory over the giant. Did David not know this? Or has he been preparing the ground all the time to acquire this very object, the symbol of his own personal power? Ahimelech is convinced by the young warrior before him.

> Take it for yourself, take – for it is right for no one but you! (v. 10).

David accepts and slips away, hoping to find temporary refuge with the Philistines.

But this episode has been observed by one of Saul's servants, Doeg the Edomite. When Saul accuses his court of being in David's pay, Doeg reveals that David was at Nob.

Is his version of what happened merely how he saw the events from outside, or is he playing up to Saul's fears of a conspiracy, seeing a chance for his own advancement?

> I saw the son of Jesse (here he borrows Saul's insulting term for David) come to Nob to Ahimelech ben Ahitov. He sought the Eternal on his behalf, gave him provisions and even gave him the sword of Goliath the Philistine (I Sam. 22.9–10).

This version makes Ahimelech a deliberate conspirator. Saul summons the priest and his household. His question is pointed and direct.

> Why have you conspired against me, you and the son of Jesse, in giving him bread and a sword and seeking God on his behalf so as to rise up and lay in wait for me as at this day? (v. 13).

Ahimelech asks a question in turn, one touched with irony for the reader, though presumably asked by the priest in all innocence.

> But who among all your servants is as faithful as David, the king's son-in-law, obedient in your service and honoured in your house? Have I begun today to seek God on his behalf? Far be it from me! Let not the king impute such a thing to his servant nor to all my father's household, for your servant knew nothing of this matter, much or little (vv. 14–15).

In Saul's state of mind, this can only mean treason. On no further evidence he pronounces an immediate sentence of death on Ahimelech and his household.

Turn about and slay the priests of the Eternal for their hand too is with David and because they knew that he was in flight and did not inform me (v. 17).

His own soldiers mutiny and refuse to kill a priest of the Eternal, But Doeg the Edomite has no such scruples. At the king's command he slays all eighty-five men present, then sacks the city of Nob killing men, women and children, cattle and sheep. One priest alone, Aviathar, a son of Ahimelech, escaped and would eventually become a loyal and faithful servant of David.

The massacre at Nob introduced a terrible escalation in the strife between the houses of Saul and David. It marked the peak of Saul's paranoia. David had the grace to admit to Aviathar his responsibility for the deaths (I Sam. 22.22).

The only ones to emerge with honour are the soldiers who refused to obey Saul's unacceptable orders – a precedent of enormous significance for the role and responsibility of an army.

The unnamed victims leave us only their story and the memory of the head of the household, a priest too unworldly for the intrigue and violence of a new epoch in Israel's troubled history.

There is a Rabbinic observation on this story that offers an interesting insight into the workings of Saul's mind. They brought this episode together with the famous story of Saul's successful battle with the Amalekites (I Sam. 15). However, against Samuel's express wishes, he spared King Agag, kept the booty and did not kill them off 'from the men to the women, from the babes to the sucklings, from the oxen to the lambs, from the camels to donkeys' (I Sam. 15.3). The command to do so is itself problematic enough, but Saul's reasons for sparing them are not because of some moral objection – rather he gave in to the wishes of his soldiers, to keep the booty for themselves. Instead of moral courage, Saul displayed a weakness in his own authority. This event marked the final break between Samuel and Saul.

However, in the story of Ahimelech, the description of the destruction of Nob follows almost word for word Samuel's instructions about the Amalekites – only the camels are missing.

And Nob, the city of the priests he (Doeg) put to the sword, from men to women, from babes to sucklings, as well as oxen, donkeys and lambs (I Sam. 22.19).

The Rabbis, in comparing Saul's behaviour on these two occasions, perhaps because of the identical wording of the destruction, simply observed:

One who is kind when he should be cruel, will end up being cruel when he should be kind.

Saul's insecurity and weakness was the issue. It led to a degree of irrationality and arbitrariness, where all judgment failed him. Fatal flaws in someone bearing the weight, responsibility and power of a king. Or as Samuel himself expressed it:

Though you are small in your own eyes, you are still the head of the tribes of Israel, and the Eternal has anointed you as king over Israel (I Sam. 15.17).

SAUL

I debated a long time about including this section. It is different from all but one of the others in being derived from another sermon at the Bendorf Bible Week. But it was not the structure of the piece, which I have more or less retained, that worried me. Nor the fact that it is not bound to a particular text or texts in the same way as the others, though I hope that it is also defensible as a legitimate piece of biblical analysis. Rather it is the 'meditative' approach to the subject of Saul, and the attempt to give a first-person insight into his experience, that gave me pause. And even that is not the whole matter, because to enter Saul's tortured life, you have to come close to his madness in some way. I tried to do this in the sermon – Bendorf is one of the few places and communities where such a thing is possible – and succeeded almost too well. Certainly some friends were most unnerved by its intensity and thought I might also have gone over the top on this occasion – aesthetically and literally! But without some risks even sermons at Bendorf can become too comfortable.

Clearly the event, and the work on Saul during the Bible Week, meant a lot to me at the time, so it deserves to be given another airing. And having already treated Saul a number of times indirectly, and almost inevitably critically, in this book (Saul's Servant, Ritzpah, Palti ben Laish, Ahimelech ben Ahitov) I owe him a chance to speak for himself.

By way of a further introduction: On the first evening of the Bible Week, when we were studying texts in the latter part of I Samuel, we divided up the conference participants into four groups as a 'warming up' exercise. Each group represented one of the major protagonists in the story – Saul, Samuel, Jonathan and David – each one a potential or actual 'king'. The purpose was that during the week of detailed study each person would try to see the events through the eyes of his or her own particular character as well as getting a general overview. I pulled 'Saul' out of the hat – and had to revise my views of him. A week later my Shabbat morning sermon included the following:

Saul, the king chosen by Samuel, comes to be rejected by God. When I first read these stories about him, I saw him through Samuel's eyes – his weakness, his irrationality – and understand why he was not fit to be king. It all seemed very clear. But during this week I have had to revise my ideas because of the game we played on the opening night. I was in the 'Saul group', so I have been forced to look more closely at this judgment of Saul and try to understand the reality of his experience.

Let me first explain things in the light of our texts and then try to speak on another level.

The game we played last Sunday led us to divide into three further groups, each representing a different aspect of power: Priest, Politician and Prophet.

In the Book of Samuel, Samuel contains within himself all three aspects. He is a prophet, speaking the word of God; he is a priest, succeeding Eli after Shiloh was destroyed; he is virtually king, as the strongest political leader in the country – and all of this without election or special anointing, because he is the last *shofet*, judge or leader, who has emerged spontaneously under God's providence to guide God's people.

Now a king is to be established and a new system, and Saul is invited to take on the role as he sees fit.

But Saul does not 'fit'. He tries to combine within himself, like Samuel, all three roles – and fails in all of them.

As a political leader he bows too readily to the will of the people (I Sam. 14.45; 15.15).

He has a prophetic gift, but it serves only as a tragic parody of what that could mean – for he stumbles between ecstasy and delirium (I Sam. 10.10–13; 18.10; 19.24), and cannot reach God when he needs to (I Sam. 14.37).

As a priest he is a strange religious figure – who orders fasts when he should order food (14.24), who sacrifices when he should not (13.8–14), who is pious when he should be practical and even tries to murder a whole priestly family (22.12–19).

Were Saul a figure in a comic tale he would be a '*schlemihl*', one who staggers from one disaster to another. But, because of the nature of the story before us, he is instead a tragic failure.

David, on the other hand, somehow fulfils the three roles and restores the balance – but in a different way from Samuel or Saul. He is indeed a powerful and astute political leader. But early in his career we hear that a prophet is a regular part of his entourage –first, of course, Samuel, but then Gad (I Sam. 22.5) and Nathan. He also acquires Abiathar (I Sam. 22.20–23; 23.6; 27.20), the last survivor of the priests of Nob murdered by Saul, to accompany him.

David knows how to delegate – he institutionalizes the three powers so that each can interact with and control the other. He is king, but with him are the priest and prophet.

So on one level Saul is a transitional figure – one who tried to continue the role played by Samuel. But if the people are to have their own king, then the will of God must be heard in another way and God's word safeguarded.

It is no accident that with the appearance of the first king, we also meet the *b'nei nevi'im*, the 'sons' or 'guild' of prophets, who are associated with Samuel. Perhaps that is also Samuel's major achievement – to create the role of the prophet as conscience of the king, answerable to no earthly powers but to God alone.

Yet for this past week I must become Saul and see the world through his eyes – a world suddenly radiant with challenge and hope, for I am anointed to be king over Israel! But a world also of darkness and dread: where every success turns to failure; where family and friends betray me; where every act of piety is rejected by God; where every move I make is hemmed in by obstacles; where every hope for the future of my dynasty is undermined; where every power I possess is stolen from me; and where even the control I have over my mind and emotions is likely to collapse at any moment: I wake to find my spear in the wall, whom have I tried to kill? I hear them whispering in the night – who is it plans to pull me down? And if God is not there to hear me, to whom can I speak, with whom share my loneliness, to whom confess my fear?

I am Saul – and a voice has spoken to me, an agent of God. I am anointed to be king. I awake to my power over others, to my control over the world about me. I am dazzled by wonder and glory. I am not just any man – God speaks to me and I am king!

I am politician – I can manipulate others and bend them to my will – by my strength, my power to dominate; or by my weakness – I am a child – protect me or I will ravage you with guilt because you have let me down.

I am priest. I can turn God to my will. I will pray Him into obedience. *Because* I know Him, if you want to know Him, you must become like me. I will have your soul. And if God does not obey me, then one of you is at fault; you have let me down, you out there are the traitor and will pay, for only I can be right.

I am prophet – only the message *I* bring from God is true. I know His will and what is for the best – for all of you out there. Why do you not listen? I will make you hear me!

I am Saul – and I am overwhelmed by the voice that has come. Can I not conquer the world? Can I not mount the heavens? Can I not create life out of death?

I am Saul – and painfully must learn that I am only a man – my power is limited, my control of my life a mirage, my knowledge a fragile cloak that covers the darkness and tumult within; my wisdom is a web of dreams to shade me from the blazing of the sun.

I am Saul – I cannot be David – he is the one that God really chose. I had my moment, but did not understand – I must die so that he may be free to serve. I cannot live after all as the Messiah – but I *can* die as Saul.

Why does God turn away His eyes? Why does He close His ears? Perhaps because I was so full, there was no room for Him. For I was king, I was the anointed one, I was *messiah*.

Though Saul's life is tragic and tortured, he conducts himself at the end with great dignity. The astonishing episode with the witch of Endor (I Sam. 28), when he conjures up the ghost of Samuel, has enormous power. It can be read as an event in outer reality. But if the figure he sees is really only a projection of his mind, then the message he gives to himself, acknowledging his past failures and recognizing his impending death, means that he has somehow come to terms with reality at the end. He goes one final time as king of Israel to fight for his people and to die.

Saul died as Saul. His life was a journey through darkness to discover who he was. Not Samuel his teacher, his 'father'; not David his pupil, his 'son'. But himself.

8

Politicians

ELNATHAN BEN ACHBOR

The Bible can be tantalizingly uninformative about someone who seems nevertheless to have an important role to play. One such person is Elnathan ben Achbor. He appears only twice, yet these two occasions are in such contradiction to each other that we become fascinated to know more about what motivated him – and nothing more is told.

He appears in those parts of the Book of Jeremiah which seem almost overly concerned with the precise recording of names. It is as if the writer were conscious of being a personal witness to events of enormous importance in the history of the nation.

What mattered was exact documentation: who was present, who saw and heard what happened, so that those who came after, perhaps even future generations, could confirm the events for themselves, or at least trust the record that was about to be handed down.

Jeremiah the prophet, deeply conscious of the approaching fall of Jerusalem to the Babylonians, constantly warned his people. For him it was not a matter of carefully calculated political alliances, or playing off the contemporary superpowers, Egypt and Babylon, against each other. What mattered was the survival of the values enshrined in their constitution as a people, the covenant with their God. The forms of that society could change, the state could be broken, the people become vassals of Babylon, such things did not matter ultimately, provided only that they managed to preserve, or recapture, the quality of life of the founding vision.

Jeremiah's lifetime was spent in trying to bring about this awareness, and for his trouble, because he was seen by the authorities as a danger, he was ridiculed, imprisoned, tortured, threatened with assassination, and, as is presumably the case here, kept under house arrest.

In an attempt to reach the people one more time, Jeremiah committed to writing all the prophecies he had received from God over the years, and sent Baruch, his friend and scribe, to read out the message of the scroll in the Temple on a public fast day (Jer. 36.1–8).

Perhaps the fast marked the initial incursions of the Babylonians into Judean territory. Certainly the public reading of such a scroll had powerful undertones, for in the days of the previous king, Josiah, the finding of a scroll during repair work on the Temple, containing the text of the covenant with God, had led to a major religious reformation. Baruch read Jeremiah's scroll.

Gemariah ben Shaphan, the Scribe, equivalent perhaps today to the Secretary of State, arranged for his son to hear the scroll read, and the latter reported to what must have been a Cabinet meeting of the government. Among those present, and therefore a high-ranking official, was Elnathan ben Achbor.

The effect of Jeremiah's scroll was very powerful, and the Ministers sent for Baruch to hear at first hand the contents, and then cross-examined Baruch to ensure that it was a faithful record of what Jeremiah had said.

Shaken by what they heard, and aware of the implications, they sent Baruch off with a warning that he and Jeremiah should go into hiding, while a delegation went to discuss the matter with King Jehoiakim. When the King heard the words of the scroll, he took a knife, cut off each piece of parchment as it was read, and burned it (Jer. 36.22–23).

His own supporters approved this act, but the delegates from the Cabinet meeting, seemingly led by Elnathan (v. 25), tried to prevent what amounted to a rejection of God's word. As they had anticipated the king tried to capture Baruch and Jeremiah, but they were well concealed.

In this dramatic way, the fate of King Jehoiakim, his régime and his people was sealed, and the story, carefully documented, was handed down by eye-witnesses who saw and felt its significance.

But what is of immediate interest is the presence among those resisting the king of Elnathan ben Achbor – because we last heard of him some chapters earlier in the Book of Jeremiah in quite different circumstances.

The episode with the scroll took place in the fourth and fifth years of the reign of Jehoiakim. In chapter 26, we are told of another occasion at the beginning of Jehoiakim's reign when Jeremiah himself spoke in the Temple, calling on the people to repent. He warned that if they did not change their ways and return to God, Jerusalem would fall and the Temple be destroyed, like the one in Shiloh had been in the days of Samuel.

The priests, the prophets and the people could not tolerate this blasphemy – was not the Temple the sacred house of the Eternal? Could God allow it to be harmed? (Though, as a careful reading of the chapter indicates, there may have been a degree of self-interest in the attempt by the priests, and the prophets, to keep Jeremiah quiet, since he was attacking the livelihood of the former and the integrity of the latter!)

Jeremiah was put on trial before the government 'princes' and the people, with the priests and prophets making the accusation, perhaps invoking the charge that he was a false prophet or had uttered blasphemy. They demanded the death penalty. Jeremiah maintained his innocence and warned that killing him would mean that innocent blood had been shed in the city, the final crime that would seal its destruction by God. Though these were important 'theological' arguments, what was at stake affected state policy and the national interest. So at a later stage in the trial, precedents to this situation were cited by both sides to underpin their argument.

For the defence the case was quoted by the elders, who presumably preserved the memory of such legal matters, of Micaiah the Morashite, who once had made a similar prophecy to that of Jeremiah in the days of King Hezekiah. This is one of the rare instances in the Bible where a prophecy from another book (Micah 3.12) is cited verbatim. In that case, runs the argument, no one demanded his death – rather the king and the people repented, and God spared Jerusalem that time (Jer. 26.17–19).

But then the prosecution produced its own more recent precedent. For a man called Uriah ben Shemaiah prophesied against the city in a similar manner to Jeremiah, and King Jehoiakim tried to execute him, but he fled to Egypt. So the king sent a diplomatic mission down to Egypt with extradition papers, brought him back and executed him (Jer. 26.20–23).

The case of Micaiah was then, runs the argument of the prosecution, but this is now. We are living in a dangerous moment, with the enemy at the door, and unlike King Hezekiah in those days, our King Jehoiakim cannot take such chances, nor can the nation as a whole bear the sort of pessimistic, subversive views that

Jeremiah is expressing. He too should die for the sake of the national interest.

This latter argument seems to have carried the day, and Jeremiah would probably have been killed had not Ahikam ben Shaphan taken him into protective custody (v. 24).

But to return to the example of what happened to Uriah ben Shemaiah: the delegation that went down to Egypt to bring him back was headed by the same Elnathan ben Achbor who would later side with Jeremiah against the king. Why had a high-ranking official like him been ready to act in the case of the extradition to support the king, yet only a short time later be part of the group fighting the king, at considerable personal risk, to ensure that the same words of prophetic warning now be heard?

There is an Achbor ben Micaiah who helped King Josiah with his religious reformation (I Kings 22.12) – perhaps he was the father of Elnathan. In which case the son followed his father into the royal service, performed his duty in the extradition matter, but then, perhaps under the influence of his father and the memory of King Josiah, realized that he had a higher responsibility even than his loyalty to the present king.

But what precisely made him change, and what became of him later, we will never know.

ELISHA BEN SHAFAT

How does one begin to understand a figure like Elisha whose life is so bound up with miraculous events and superhuman powers? At his word a barren woman can conceive (II Kings 4.16); at his curse bears attack young children (II Kings 3.24); with his prayer he can make his servant see chariots of fire surrounding them (II Kings 6.17) – and blind the eyes of raiding enemy soldiers (II Kings 6.18); with a few loaves of bread he can feed a hundred men (II Kings 4.43); with a handful of salt purify poisoned water (II Kings 2.21). He is gifted with extraordinary talents.

'Gifted' or 'cursed'? He is a 'man of God', a 'prophet', a 'holy man' and a healer. But his powers seem to cut him off from contact with his fellows. When he speaks to people he uses an intermediary – to the woman who gives him a home (II Kings 4.12–15) and to Naaman the Aramean general come to be cured of 'leprosy' (II Kings 5.10–11). In the former case he might have felt the need to be separated from a woman on ritual grounds, or to avoid social stigma – and in the latter he may have been preserving the dignity of prophecy against the arrogant assumptions of a foreign general. But perhaps the mysterious and disturbing episode of the bears was a shock to Elisha and he felt the need to be exceptionally cautious in his relationships with people from then on.

He went up from there towards Beth El and as he was going up along the way some 'young men' came out from the city and mocked him saying: 'Go up, baldy! Go up baldy!' He turned back, looked at them and cursed them in the name of the Eternal. Then two bears came out from the wood and broke them apart, forty-two children (II Kings 2.23–24).

Who the 'young men' (literally 'little men') were is not clear. The Hebrew phase could mean 'young children' or 'youths', but it might also be related to the use of '*naar*' as a servant, even 'apprentice' or 'disciple', to a prophet.

What did they intend with 'Go up, baldy!'? Hair was important to the Israelites – to cut someone's hair or beard off was an insult to his manhood. Leaving one's hair uncut was part of a religious vow (Num. 6.5). Elijah, Elisha's teacher, was recognized as a 'master of hair' (II Kings 1.8), presumably with long flowing locks, so that to call his successor, who had inherited the mantle of Elijah's power, 'baldy', was to denigrate not only Elisha but the whole prophetic office. Since Elijah had disappeared by going up to heaven in a chariot of fire, to say to Elisha 'Go up!' may have been a further insult to his status and powers.

In anger Elisha cursed them – and such was the power of his word that the bears attacked. Maybe Elisha learnt about the dangers of his powers from that experience, for it is after this that we find intermediaries standing between himself and others, perhaps to protect them.

When Elisha was called by Elijah he took on the task not completed by his master, to anoint a certain Hazael as king of Aram (I Kings 19.15). A number of stories in II Kings tell of the chronic state of hostility between Israel and Aram. There are constant border raids into Israelite territory. When Naaman, the Aramean general, comes to the king of Israel seeking a cure for his 'leprosy', the king's first assumption is that this is a pretext to make trouble (II Kings 5.7). Indeed war breaks out at one stage with a disastrous siege of Samaria, the capital (II Kings 6.24).

Yet Elisha seems to be pursuing his own separate strategy independent of state policy. When the king of Aram sends soldiers to capture Elisha, the soldiers are struck blind and led to Samaria. Rather than allow them to be killed, Elisha insists that they be well-treated and fed and then released back to their home (II Kings 6.21–23). Perhaps he has the right psychological understanding of events because the border raids cease.

If Elisha is seeking a relationship with the Arameans, the episode with Naaman may make sense in a new light. Elisha refuses to accept payment for curing Naaman, which may be a recognition that it was God's work alone. But when Gehazi, Elisha's servant, extracts the payment from Naaman by guile, Elisha's anger is expressed in quite specific terms: 'This is not the time . . . ' (II Kings 5.26). Does Elisha have in mind the power he now has over Naaman for future favours of greater importance than mere financial gain – perhaps once more of a political nature?

In the third episode where he plays a direct political role the tragic climax of Elisha's engagement with affairs of state emerges. He visits Damascus at a time when the king, Ben Hadad, is ill. His aide, Hazael, is sent to ask the prophet on behalf of the king: 'Will I recover from this illness?' Elisha, in a disturbingly ambiguous sentence, replies:

> Tell him 'You will surely recover', but the Eternal has shown me he will die (II Kings 8.10).

Then Elisha weeps, for he sees that Hazael will become king and attack Israel, destroying cities, killing children and pregnant women. Is this to be the final result of God's command to Elijah, his master, to anoint Hazael? Indeed Hazael returns to Ben Hadad and tells him he will recover. But the next sentence recounts the death of the king, possibly smothered by Hazael, who may have acted through what he felt was divine encouragement mediated by the prophet.

Elisha has the last word, if not on Hazael, then on his son. In his final prophecy he promises Joash, king of Israel, that God will bring salvation from Aram (II Kings 13.17) and indeed Joash recovers the cities lost to the Arameans (II Kings 13.25).

Elisha remains an engimatic figure. He can unleash destructive powers, but can also heal. His political activities seem to be aimed at creating peace but are doomed to failure, at least in his lifetime. Even his death gives him no peace. In a final macabre episode his bones restore to life a corpse that falls into his grave (II Kings 13.20–21)! If Elijah his master went living up to heaven, then the powers of Elisha go on living beneath the earth.

AHITOPHEL

It is a favourite scene. The hero confronts the villain, weapons at the ready. The odds seem stacked on the side of the villain. The first move gives him an even greater advantage, but at the last moment the hero brings out a final reserve of strength or speed and wins. A variant on the theme does not require physical weapons, but rather a battle of wits.

Rarely is the duel so clearly portrayed as in the struggle between Ahitophel the Gilonite and Hushai the Archite – at stake, the future of the kingdom of Israel under David or Absalom (II Sam. 15.1– 17.23).

Absalom, David's beloved son, rebelled against him. Immediately after making his first move, he sent for Ahitophel, described as David's counsellor, one of the highest rank of policy-makers.

Why he joined the conspiracy is not clear. Two brief genealogical notes show that he is the father of Eliam, and that is the same name as Bathsheba's father. So Ahitophel might have been upset by the family scandal about his granddaughter and David.

But there is quite another possibility. Ahitophel seems to be a sort of thinking machine, a man of such clear perception of the way events will work out that it is said of him:

> Now in those days the counsel which Ahitophel gave was as if one consulted the word of God (II Sam. 16.23).

He stood outside private commitment or subjective judgments or even a particularly moral view of affairs. His strength lay in the objectivity he brought to his opinions.

Given the situation, he could predict the best course of events to follow, with unerring accuracy, on behalf of the one who asked the questions. To his dispassionate view of things, with David's gradually weakening power and control over events, it was indeed time for the eldest son, Absalom, to take over.

Such is the cleverness of Absalom's opening moves in the coup that it might be that Ahitophel's hand is already behind them. Absalom took two hundred leading citizens, ignorant of the plot, from Jerusalem with him to perform a sacrificial ceremony. This put them under Absalom's control and at the same time made them appear to be suspect to David.

He declared his kingdom in Hebron, David's first capital, at one blow cutting off from David any help from Judah, the one part of the country that might be expected to support him. By having messengers announce Absalom's takeover at the same time throughout the country, it seemed as if the whole thing was over, thus winning the propaganda war by controlling the media.

Whether all this was Ahitophel's doing or not, he was now part of Absalom's entourage. Against this phenomenal mind, David sent back to Jerusalem his friend Hushai to offer his services to Absalom and try to foil his plans.

Absalom's immediate problem is how to dispose of David. Ahitophel advises:

> Let me choose twelve thousand men, and I will set out and pursue David tonight. I will come upon him while he is weary and discouraged, and throw him into a panic; and then all the people who are with him will flee. I will strike down the king only, and I will bring all the people back to you . . . (II Sam. 17.1–3)

The plan is impeccable and likely to succeed. It would mean catching David before he had time to gain supporters and re-group. By making it clear that they were interested only in the person of David, others who were weak in their support might defect.

In Ahitophel's readiness to lead the soldiers himself there are two further advantages: Absalom is left at the centre of events to strengthen his hold on the country; and the dirty work of disposing of David is left to another, which can allow Absalom a degree of 'deniability' for what happens to his father should he ever need it. However, the very presence of Ahitophel at the head of twelve thousand soldiers could also hint at a degree of personal glory-seeking. And though that seems entirely out of character it provides a peg for Hushai to fasten on to when asked his view of the plan.

Hushai comes straight out against it:

> The policy which Ahitophel advises is not good in this particular case. You know that your father and his men are mighty men, and that they are bitterly angry, like a bear robbed of her cubs in the field. Besides, your father is a man of war and will not spend the night with the troops.

Behold, by now he has hidden himself in one of the pits or in some other place, and when he falls on (his pursuers) first, whoever hears it will say, 'there has been a great disaster among Absalom's followers!' Then even the bravest man, with the heart of a lion, will melt with fear, for all Israel knows what a warrior your father is and that those with him are mighty men.

But my advice would be that all Israel, from Dan to Beersheba, be gathered to you, like the sand by the sea for multitude, and that you go in person into battle. So we shall come upon him in some place where he is to be found, and we shall fall upon him as the dew falls upon the ground; and of him and of all the men with him not a single one will be left.

In response to Ahitophel's self-assurance in explaining his tactics, Hushai's approach makes it seem that Absalom himself is the one who is making the decisions: '*You* know what your father is like . . .' He stresses David's power, which both flatters Absalom's own courage in taking on David, but also reinforces the fears of losing the support of the people if there are any setbacks.

To counter these fears, he comes up with the idea of delaying until a magnificent army has gathered, thus apparently giving Absalom the necessary overwhelming strength, but also giving David time to prepare and choose his own ground.

Hushai crowns this by the glorious image of the handsome Absalom at the head of this mighty army riding off to fight, which must appeal to Absalom's well-known vanity.

In response to Ahitophel's original plan, the text says:

The matter was right in the eyes of Absalom and in the eyes of all the elders of Israel (II Sam. 17.4).

This would suggest that some degree of discussion ensued with senior advisers and the plan was accepted. After Hushai's proposal, the text simply says:

Then Absalom said, and all the men of Israel, 'Better is the plan of Hushai the Archite than the plan of Ahitophel' (II Sam. 17.14).

This seems to imply that it was Absalom who responded to the plan and a lot of his courtiers instantly agreed. Absalom has fallen for the logic of the argument, and the neatly insinuated flattery. Hushai wins.

The result is well-known. David takes advantage of the delay won for him by Hushai, gathers his forces and defeats Absalom who gets caught in a tree by his beautiful, long hair, the symbol of his vanity.

But what of Ahitophel?

He brings that same impeccable logic to bear upon his own situation. Recognizing in the acceptance of Hushai's plan the inevitable defeat of Absalom, and his own subsequent disgrace, he acts with great dignity, ensuring the security of his family.

> When Ahitophel saw that his policy was not followed, he saddled his ass, arose and went home to his city. He set his house in order, and hanged himself. He died and was buried in the grave of his fathers (II Sam. 17.23).

AMAZIAH

Amaziah, the Priest of Beth El, thought he knew how to deal with troublemakers. That much we learn from the few verses that speak of him in the book of the prophet Amos.

The episode happened during a short period of apparent calm and success amidst the stormy history of the northern kingdom of Israel. Whereas the southern kingdom of Judah remained constant to the house of David for four centuries, in the two hundred years of its existence, Israel had twenty kings, of which only two managed to create dynasties that lasted for more than two generations.

During the thirty-year reign of Jeroboam II there was a marked material success for the kingdom. Their chief northern enemy, Syria, was in decline and the country expanded to recapture lost territories and reached the dimensions it once had under Solomon.

Enormous wealth became available, partly through Israel's control of the major trade routes through the region. The gap between rich and poor increased greatly, with the wealthy buying up the family lands of the poor and reducing them to virtual slavery. But within twenty-five years of the death of Jeroboam II, and six kings later, the kingdom fell under the control of the Assyrians.

Religion under Amaziah the priest was also very successful, if measured by the enormous number of sacrifices performed at his sanctuary, the high attendance of worshippers at every feast day, new moon and Sabbath, and the beautiful music that accompanied the rituals; all paid for, in the view of Amos, by the ruthless exploitation of the poor.

Amos of Tekoa, from the southern kingdom of Judah, spoke out against the injustice in the northern kingdom. In a startling series of visions (Amos 7.1–9 8.1–3) he saw that dangers looming over the nation were such that they threatened to destroy it.

Each time he prayed to God to withold the danger, and the threat was withdrawn. But then came a vision of a plumbline held over the nation, perhaps to force the prophet himself to measure the degree of corruption. With that judgment clear, the prophet knew that the end was at hand and set about warning the people of what their future might be.

At this point he came into conflict with the priest of Beth El, the royal sanctuary originally set up as a rival to Jerusalem when the northern kingdom seceded after Solomon's death.

In one of his oracles, Amos had proclaimed in God's name:

The high places of Isaac shall be made desolate and the sanctuaries of Israel shall be laid waste, and I will rise against the house of Jeroboam with the sword (Amos 7.9).

Perhaps his words picked up a mood in the general populace because in panic Amaziah sent word to the king denouncing the prophet.

Amos has conspired against you in the midst of the house of Israel; the land is not able to bear his words (Amos 7.10).

Of Amos's warnings about the destruction of the sanctuaries nothing is said. Perhaps Amaziah assumed he would be more effective by drawing the king's attention to the threat against the régime rather than against the religious institutions. For this purpose he even appears to distort the prophet's message so that it looks like a personal attack on the king – the prophet referred to 'the house of Jeroboam', the régime itself; Amaziah claims 'Amos has conspired against you'.

The Bible does not record an answer from the king on the subject of this troublesome prophet – for which later Rabbinic tradition was to give him some credit. If there was no official response, then perhaps Amaziah has rightly guessed that the king does not think too highly of his senior religious authority and the priest is left to deal with the prophet personally.

His opening words to Amos are clearly dismissive:

O seer, go flee for your own good to the land of Judah, and there eat your bread, and there do your prophesying! Never again prophesy in Beth El, for it is the royal sanctuary and the temple of the kingdom! (Amos 7.12–13).

The word 'seer', *hozeh*, derives from a verb meaning 'to see', used in more poetic texts, and may have referred originally to one who had visions. It came to be one of a number of terms in use for a 'prophet'. It may even have been the specific title for a prophet attached to the royal palace to provide oracles and advice for the king – so that in using this term, Amaziah is implying that Amos has been sent up north as a professional agitator by the southern king. Hence the suggestion that he 'eat his bread' there, a technical term referring to those who were financially supported by the king, who 'ate at the royal table'.

He might also be implying that 'down south' they may quite like to hear prophecies about the destruction of the northern kingdom, but that such views were not wanted in Beth El. The word 'flee' adds a threat – it may not be safe to stay here.

Finally, he asserts all his authority as the religious leader of the country, priest of the royal sanctuary, and hence with the entire power of the kingdom behind his words: 'never again prophesy at Beth El!'

Amos replies with the famous statement:

I am no prophet, nor the son of a prophet. I am a cattle herder and a tender of sycamore trees. But the Eternal took me from following the flock and the Eternal said to me: 'Go, prophesy to My people Israel' (7.14–15).

He asserts that he is no 'professional prophet' – the phrase 'son of a prophet' probably means a 'disciple' of a prophet who would in turn prophesy. (Hence the 'sons of the prophets' who accompanied Elisha – II Kings 4.38.) Moreover he is no king's agent – his only master is God.

Amos goes on to spell out to Amaziah the implications of God's warning of destruction to that entire society – by applying them directly to the unfortunate priest himself.

You say, 'do not prophesy against Israel, do not preach against the House of Isaac!'. Therefore, thus says the Eternal: Your wife will become a harlot in the city and your sons and your daughters will fall by the sword, and your land will be divided up by a measuring string, and in an unclean land you will die and Israel will be exiled from their land! (Amos 7.17).

It is *Amaziah*'s wife who will have to earn her livelihood as a whore, *his* sons and daughters who will be killed, and *he* is the one who will die on unclean territory – away from the 'sacred' Beth El, or in a Beth El defiled by the invaders.

No more is heard of Amaziah. Presumably his world was destroyed, as Amos warned, when Israel fell to the Assyrians. Only his bluster remains and the defensive manipulations of outraged authority – a spiritual leader who believed in his own power and could not risk hearing the word of God.

KING AHAZ

The following section requires a little explanation. It was not created as a 'Bible Lives' piece but was originally a sermon at the annual Jewish-Christian Bible Week in Bendorf, Germany, the second year that we had dealt with the Book of Isaiah. Having spoken about the prophet in the previous year,[1] it seemed only fair to examine King Ahaz with whom he was in conflict.

Isaiah 7 records one of their arguments and Ahaz appears to be somewhat hypocritical, suddenly pretending to be overly pious and not wishing to 'test God', v. 12, even though the prophet offers him the chance of a miraculous sign. But though we tend to identify with the prophet, I found myself in sympathy with King Ahaz. After all, he thought he was dealing with political 'realities', and the prophet was offering him seemingly unrealizable divine promises. Though it is important not to make the mistake of assuming that Isaiah's views are merely 'pie in the sky' and not rooted in practicalities as well. The prophets did not exist in some sort of religious vacuum divorced from politics.

So the following is a word of support (if occasionally a little ironic) for Ahaz and all the other biblical kings who found themselves bewildered by the demands of God as expressed by provocative prophets.

I have great sympathy for King Ahaz. Kings have to deal with reality

---

[1]The sermon is included in *A Rabbi's Bible*, pp. 92–97 in a chapter called 'Risking – the Bible and Creativity'.

as they see it. They must take responsibility for their society, for improving the gross national product, for curbing inflation, for ensuring the maintenance of basic services, for balancing the interests of the different social and political factions, negotiating, compromising, holding the ring. They must master the art of expediency.

They must also ensure that the structure, integrity and values of the national religion are maintained. The clergy must be adequately supported and all appropriate Temples, shrines and secondary institutions kept in a state of repair and functioning. They must also keep a strict control over the more extravagant demands of the faithful. High Priests and Court Prophets need to be representative figures, people of diplomacy, tact, practical wisdom. People who know the place of religion in the scheme of things, and who can guarantee the behaviour of their adherents.

Kings must also ensure the continuity of their régime and take appropriate steps both to produce children and establish a clear hierarchical order of succession.

Above all they must be concerned about the integrity of borders, which means the maintenance of a standing army, properly equipped with the latest weapons, fed and housed. For this, of course, they require a guaranteed revenue, which, as David and Solomon discovered, requires adequate demographic studies, a taxation system and a full bureaucratic back-up. This in turn means appropriate education structures and resources to provide a pool of literate people from which to select your functionaries and ensure their further training, as well as communication systems throughout the country, methods of enforcing tax collecting and hence a proper state-controlled judiciary.

All of which is in turn dependent upon prevailing international conditions, on the correct and appropriate relationships with all bordering and neighbouring states. This is naturally the most taxing of work, given the number and relative instability of the various countries surrounding Judah, let alone the subtle ambiguities of living with the other half of the divided kingdom, Israel, with its inevitable rivalries and disturbing similarities.

Border disputes being a commonplace, an international system of law and a language of diplomacy need to be mastered, as well as subscribing to some supranational system for judging the rights and wrongs of a given case. Clearly trade requirements, natural historical affinities with particular nations, mutual political or religious goals must lead to short-term or long-term alliances – and the danger of political adventures as one or more nation gains particular power or sees the chance of a quick gain of territory at the expense of another. All of which is further confused by the awareness of the strategic significance of the kingdoms of Israel and Judah to the super-powers to the north and south, which frequently expanded or contracted at the expense of the small states in the region. For Israel and Judah stood at the meeting place of three land masses and three oceans, in physical control of two crucial land routes. They were clearly a tempting prize for any nation with imperial aspirations.

It is not easy to be a king of Israel or Judah. I have great sympathy for King Ahaz.

These realities are also addressed by Isaiah in his description of the ideal king (Isaiah 11). For he will be invested with a spirit that comes from God: a spirit of wisdom (as taught in the schools of international diplomacy) and understanding (the ability to discriminate that is vital to a judicial role); a spirit of counsel (the technical term for political policy-making) and a spirit of power (for, above all, temporal power resides with the earthly king). He is to be the ideal leader, the magisterial captain of the complex ship of state.

There is no magic or sentimentality in this description. It addresses the brute reality of government and power. It is political truth. Isaiah is no anarchist.

And yet Isaiah hears another voice as well. It is a voice that demands a different set of values and it drives him out of the hierarchy of power which was his by right into political and social isolation. It is a passion for social justice. Not for a judicial system alone, but for one which ensures that the rights of the poor and underprivileged are maintained. One which redresses the financial and social imbalances that accompany the successful economic expansion of the kingdom.

For Isaiah the covenant, as the blueprint for society given by God, is a reflection of the unique, awesome and holy God. It is this transcendent, other, different, special God who imprints upon Isaiah an awareness of the awful gap between the ideal society under the covenant and the pragmatic materialism of Judah under King Ahaz. And when this gap between the ideal and the real was too great, then somehow destruction must come. For the God of Israel was a jealous God, a passionate God, one who would not stand idly by when the values of the covenant were ignored or abused. Who or what might bring the destruction mattered little, its inevitability haunted the prophet.

Isaiah's political isolationism – make no alliances with Syria or Israel, do not turn to Assyria, do not welcome the representatives of Babylon – all these elements belong to an awareness of the futility of such political manoeuvres. Even building the defences and strengthening the army were pointless exercises. God had marked the nation for destruction and nothing they now did could prevent it. The only consolation, as he proclaimed in the most dramatic way by the naming of his children, was that a remnant would return to start again. At some future date, the people would again say: *Imanu El* – God is with us.

Yet how to square the realities of running a kingdom, of holding together all its disparate forces so that it can function in the most effective way, with this challenge for justice, for a quality of life for all people and a true expression of the will of God?

Isaiah could do no more than point to the need to try and hold together these two realities. In his description of the ideal king, he prefaced and sealed his list of qualities with two more. On this king would rest first of all the *ruach adonay*, the spirit of the Eternal. Then come the human, practical qualities of kingship – Wisdom and understanding; counsel and power. But at the end, to seal these qualities come two more: the spirit of *da'at*, knowledge as personal experience and *yirat adonai*, the fear and awe of God.

This ideal king must rule between boundaries determined by the *spirit* of the Eternal, which invests him with his gifts, and the *fear* of the Eternal that tests and judges day by day the use to which he puts them. To all his other burdens, this king must match his pragmatism to his religious faith, his fear of the nations of the world to his fear of God, Creator of his nation and of all others.

It is, of course, an almost impossible task. Which is why, in Jewish tradition at least, no human being has yet achieved it. We have known many messianic pretenders, but none has succeeded.

Against such an array of expectations poor Ahaz had no chance.

9

Purim Spiels

ON BEN PELET

As I suggested in my introduction the following two passages about On ben Pelet were created as spoofs – the first for a Purim edition of the *Jewish Chronicle*, the second during a rather solemn Bible scholars' conference as a defence against incipient boredom. They parody two different approaches to biblical scholarship – the 'historical-critical school' and the 'narrative art' school. However, I must confess that my style here is a little bit over the top – though in the case of the 'narrative art school' it is not that far removed from the real thing. Since I could not let well alone, some of the alphabetically listed comments towards the end are almost serious. I have also used the same idea to conclude both pieces, but added an extra nuance to the second one.

The joke at the heart of this exercise is the mysterious reference to one On ben Pelet as a co-conspirator with Korach in his rebellion against Moses (Num. 16) – see the sections above on 'Korach' and on 'Dathan and Abiram' for further details. However, whereas the fate of all the other conspirators is mentioned, On appears only in the opening verse and is never mentioned again. So what happened to him? That is the real mystery, to which the following two pieces offer an indication of how different scholarly approaches might deal with him.

For the record, the Rabbis offered a solution. When On went home that night after agreeing to join with Korach, his wife told him off. 'If you stick with Moses', she pointed out, 'you have no special position or prominence, but if you join with Korach, you'll still have no special position or prominence – so you're better off leaving the whole business alone!'

'But', replied the miserable On, 'I've already promised Korach I'd be there in the morning!'

So his wife slipped something into his drink which put him to sleep so that he did not wake up in time in the morning. When someone came to summon him to the meeting, his wife sat in the entrance to the tent, with her hair hanging down which implied that she was in a very disturbed state. This so unnerved the messenger that he came no nearer – and On managed to sleep through the rebellion and survive unharmed.

So much for the midrash, now for the 'scholars'.

1. *Prolegomenon to a source-critical analysis of the On ben Pelet Pericope in Numbers 16*

Few biblical figures have aroused such controversy as On Ben Pelet. Clearly, he was a man of enormous significance to the Israelite community, to be listed among the leaders of the wilderness period. Yet the very paucity of information about him, the tantalizing puzzle that surrounds his fate, and indeed the utter confusion into which the cryptic reference to him has thrown the scholarly world, add romance and excitement to the quest to find his true identity. More than three thousand years after his death the fateful name of On Ben Pelet (Num. 16.1) weaves its magic spell upon us still today.

Scholarly opinion, in its quest for sources to the Pentateuchal narratives, is strongly divided between those who advocate a separate 'O' (for On) source and others who equally forcibly contend that we must consider a 'Pelet' codex.

Supporters of the 'On' source theory draw upon what they consider the earliest reference to the name, in the extended form 'Onan', son of Judah, who, according to Genesis 38.3–10, had a premature extermination because of his refusal to provide offspring to his deceased brother's widow, Tamar.

The 'On school' perceptively recognizing in the Genesis narrative a disguised account of the extinction, in the early days of the Israelite tribal league, of the tribe of Onan, suggest that a handful of survivors remained and left this cryptic clue to their continued existence in the Numbers passage.

Thus, the fact that 'On' joined the rebellion of Korach against Moses means that the surviving members of the Onan tribe, enraged at the indiscriminate writing out of history of their illustrious ancestor in the official record, have put this secret note into the tale to indicate their continued existence.

They derive evidence for this theory from the second part of the name – 'Pelet', amending it by replacing the final letter *tav* with the letter '*tet*', alleging a scribal error during dictation. This corrected word gives a root meaning to 'escape' or 'deliver'. Hence the phrase 'On Ben Pelet' means literally, 'On, son of freedom', or, more accurately, 'On is in the category of those who have escaped'. The message of the reference in Numbers is thus abundantly clear: 'Onan lives!!'

While distinguished scholars have lent their names to this hypothesis, it must be noted that there are equally learned and staunch supporters of the 'Pelet codex' theory. Here attention has been drawn to the mysterious 'mercenary soldiers' of King David, known as *hacreti v'hapleti*, the Cherethites and Pelethites, or Cretans and Philistines.

In an interpretation that has entered the scholarly world as 'the Pelethite conspiracy', the references to David's Pelethite mercenaries hides the true leadership of the Israelite nation at this crucial time of transition from tribal chieftains (judges) to the first kings.

Where, the argument runs, could a small, red-haired, womanizing poet like David have acquired the skill and power to mould the divided semi-loyal tribal agglomerations, euphemistically called by Saul a 'kingdom', into a strong nation and empire?

The answer must be sought in David's 'missing years', when he lived among the Philistines, who alone of all the peoples in the region, had the statescraft and military expertise to conceive such a strategy. Under their tutelage, and allegedly supported, but actually manipulated, by the force of trained Pelethite social engineers, David's every move in his rise to the throne was brilliantly plotted.

Such was their power and their desire to maintain secrecy that they were instrumental in the writing of the 'official' history of the period that has come down to us in the so-called 'Book of Samuel', taking pains to hide every trace of their machiavellian ordering of events.

So thorough was their work of concealment that it was not until this century that the extent of their influence was revealed through a brilliant, if controversial, piece of scholarship that unearthed the true meaning of the stories in 'Samuel' about 'Palti (sic) ben Laish'.

According to the official version, Saul, in his anger with David, took Michal his daughter from David and gave her to Palti, David only retrieving her after Saul's death. A close reading reveals that no such person as Palti really existed and this entire story is an allegory to indicate that the true Israel (Michal) had been taken out of the hands of its rightful rulers (Saul and David) and given over to the power of the Pelethites.

The proof of this can be found in a key provided by the ingenious scribal author in his anachronistic reference in II Samuel 21.8 to Michal being married to one Adriel ben Barzilai. Clearly, the Pelethite censors overlooked this hint at the truth that lay hidden until now. Since Michal could not have been married to yet a third husband, it is clear that this name is also a code, and, knowing what lies behind it, it is a simple matter to translate it as the 'flock' (*eder*) of 'God' (*el*), that is, Israel, is under 'iron' (*barzel*), is enchained by the Pelethites.

Hence the name 'On Ben Pelet' was inserted by the Pelethites into the Book of Numbers out of some private conceit – for 'On' means 'power', and the name really means 'Pelet rules!'

Such was the state of scholarship until a recent discovery in a cave in Qumran exploded both theories. For among the tiny fragments preserved and painstakingly restored by a team of archaeologists at the Hebrew University was a piece that clearly contained the closing words of the Book of Numbers.

But appended to them in the same scribal hand was the following sentence which resolves all questions about how the name got into scripture:

> The author wishes to acknowledge the research fellowship of the On Ben Pelet Memorial Foundation without which this scroll could never have been written.

2. *Who knows 'On'? Towards a deconstructive reading of Numbers 16.1c*
Protasis

He emerges out of conflict and disappears into silence. Neither anonymous nor fully identifiable, he is the repository of our projections, the quintessential gap. On Ben Pelet – the witness to conspiracies, representative of the bewildered common person, a bystander in the struggle of leaders, bemused, compromised, yet eternally present.

And then his disappearance. Was it before the purge or after? Is he Schweik, the eternal survivor, too shrewd to be caught in the arena? Or is he the victim of that pride and ambition that puts vanity above the cause, that relishes an association with the manipulators

of power, that places hand-me-down glory before common sense?
Does On slink away, or sink into the earth, or rise to heaven as a
blazing offering? Is he actor or prop? An afterthought or the
ultimate focus of attention, his troubling, specified anonymity
transfixing the reader by its irrelevance, redundancy?

Without On there is no story. The interwoven complexity of
plotters, confused in their interrelationships and motivations and
pre-eminence falls apart without that focussing point. For On is the
audience (*Zuhörerschaft*) that gives Korach power and Moses
authority. Out of the crowd he emerges giving it depth and reality,
social form and ominous weight. What is at stake, the saving of an
entire people, the transformation of a world, depends upon their
correct reading of these events, their commitment crystalized and
personified in the ambigious On.

When titans clash the people tremble, the wise retire and
opportunists multiply.

His name reveals much or nothing. He comes of the doomed and
troubled tribe of Reuben. 'On' signifies 'vigour', 'power'. Is that the
authority to which he was born? to which he aspired? Or an ironic
joke at his expense, the one of thwarted ambition?

'Ben Pelet', by an inevitable word play, becomes the 'escaped
one'. Child of the generation born in the twilight of Egyptian
bondage, dedicated to liberation but doomed to wander in the
eternal wilderness. A lifetime's hopes invested in the son – perhaps
the next generation could finally make it – or the next or the next.
The name breathes expectation and recoils against the bitter reality
of failed promises, failed hope, the despairing gesture of rebellion.

Yet On is not alone. He stands amidst the ranks of similar figures,
anonymous yet deeply, deeply impressive, burning themselves into
the biblical consciousness through their very unknownness, un-
knowableness: the man who showed Joseph the way; Jacob's
midnight opponent; and, above all, the betrayed and cheated Ploni,
pre-eminent as the greedy dupe, primed, propositioned and pre-
empted through Boaz's classic connivance. The named man without
a role meets here in perfect symmetry the man with a role but no
name, a dialectic of defeat, point-counterpoint, two cruxes, ineff-
able in their otherness, tautologous in their analogic unity.

We gasp at the daring of this juxtaposition, this exemplary
conceit. On, who holds by the merest fingertips on to the coat-tails
of history, the decisive figure in the Moses/Korach struggle, whose
choice one way or the other damns or redeems incipient Israel;

Ploni, the eternal might-have-been, the all-but, the almost-made-it, who missed out on the greatest conceivable honour, to sire a messianic line. What fortunate heppenstance got On included in; what hapless fate got Ploni written out?

And yet is this not too precipitate? For much as On is the antonym of Ploni, the threads of analogy lead us inevitably, unfailingly, irreversibly elsewhere.

For On, the mute witness, the silent one, the martyred one, prefigures that other mysterious, nameless one, pain-wracked and tortured, dumb in his suffering, supernal in his inevitable vindication, the Servant of the Eternal. Overlooked, not estimated, a figure of laughter and scorn, who holds in his very silence and anonymity the key to redemption, divine grace and will. The doomed, martyred, speechless On reaches out across the centuries to meet his unknown descendant; the type too of the saintly ones, unknown and unacknowledged, of later tradition, the *lamed-vavniks*, the mute ones, the 'thirty-six' just ones for whose sake and whose sake alone the world is permitted to continue. And deeper still, almost as an afterthought, we find the excluded feminine other of gender defective biblical self-deception.

Apodosis

And yet may it not be argued that we are venturing here a little beyond the evidence? The On of myth and legend, the On Ben Pelet who glides silently through the unconscious of authors, redactors and canonizers alike, to explode out of the pages of Numbers, is this an On we can seriously contemplate? How do we control such rich material, such surplus of meaning? Where, we must ask, does the harvest begin to tread on the heels of the planter?

(*a*) On is textually well attested.[1] His seeming irrelevance and subsequent disappearance confirm his legitimacy – the more unlikely text is the more probable. None of the suggested emendations successfully resolve the inherent problems. Moreover, where this particular text in Numbers seeks to conceal an identity (the two hundred and fifty leaders of the community, called to assemblies, men of renown) it has no hesitation in so doing. The very non-anonymity of On makes him the eponymous on-looker.

(*b*) The possibility of figures who witness events, who are not direct actors but whose presence helps ground and focus our attention is otherwise well attested e.g. the young men who

---

[1]Onomastically, On is seemingly related to Onan, likewise a seminal figure.

accompany Abraham to the *akeda*, the binding of Isaac, and those who join Balaam on his journey to King Balak.[2] They are normative life, humdrum, banal, ambiguous, unseeing witnesses to transcendence, us and yet not-us in our privileged status as reader.

(*c*) The complementarity of On and Ploni is admittedly more speculative – nevertheless it must be noted that the Book of Ruth draws heavily on the patriarchal narratives (the choosing of Abraham; Judah and Tamar) and focusses with great deliberation on the setting up and tricking of Ploni. As failed participants in historically significant moments, On and Ploni are structurally identical.

(*d*) The image of suffering, silent ones can be traced in an almost direct line through Michal's Palti; to the *aniyyim/annivim* of Psalms and the prophets; the mute Job of the prologue; Jeremiah's confessions, before he speaks; and the songs of the Servant. Who can tell where this archetypal figure first finds its expression in biblical thought?

(*e*) The image of the invisible yet present other, noted but not perceived as acting, is so clearly a subversive gesture that we may legitimately postulate a woman as the creator of this rich, multi-dimensional character, a view reinforced by the significant omission of any evidence whatsoever for this hypothesis.

Postscript

There remains a simpler explanation of the entire On phenomenon. It is offered with a degree of hesitation as it risks being a projection into the past of contemporary values.

We are made aware throughout the text of Exodus of the fabled generosity of the Israelites. When asked to build a tabernacle they gave with a boundless zeal. When likewise asked to create a Golden Calf, they did not stint of their golden ornaments. But among all the taxes and tithes recorded as being necessary for the maintenance of the cultus and priestly ranks, nothing is said about payment for the actual documenting and recording of Israel's sacred scripture. Perhaps when that bill had to be paid, one man stepped forward to offer the money – but on one condition. That they record his name in the book. What, one may legitimately ask, did On have to pay to get his name included? Conversely, how much more did Ploni have to pay to keep his name out?

[2]The first such 'anonymous other' may be the paradoxical figure who might kill Cain (Gen. 4.14) in an otherwise, but for his parents, unpopulated world. (David Clines, in a personal communication.)

PLONI ALMONI

As mentioned in the section on Boaz there is an unnamed character in chapter four of the Book of Ruth, the 'redeemer' who refused to take up the option of acquiring the field of Naomi for fear of ruining his family. The Hebrew term that is used for him is 'Ploni Almoni', and in line with the biblical use of that phrase (for example, in I Sam. 21.3 it means 'somewhere or other') it came to be used in Rabbinic sources as a substitute name whenever anonymity was to be preserved, the equivalent to 'John Smith' or 'John Doe'. The fact of his anonymity serves a double purpose in 'Ruth'. First it enables his identity to be kept secret lest some shame or embarrassment be permanently attached to his family. But it also achieves the ironic purpose of blotting out the family name of someone who was not prepared to preserve the family name of his relative, which was actually his religious duty.

However, there is another way of reading the story, and I took such a liberty one Purim. For some reason I found it necessary to parody yet again a sort of 'biblical-scholarly' style. For the record there is one technical term and two weak puns that need explaining. A 'Beth Din' is a Rabbinic court that decides whether a potential convert should be accepted, essentially on the religious sincerity of their motives – there are considerable arguments in the Jewish world about which Beth Din is prepared to accept the rulings of another in this delicate matter. 'Rashi' is, of course, the great mediaeval French Jewish Bible commentator; 'Pshat' is a term for the 'plain' or 'straightforward' (though not necessarily the 'literal') meaning of a text.

It was clearly a cover-up. But whom do you have to see and what do you have to pay to keep your name out of the Bible? It is only the rise of the socio-economic and anthropological studies, made possible by the revolution in computer techniques, that has raised questions like this to the forefront of biblical scholarship.

What was Moses' salary or Vashti's credit rating? Did Balaam charge mileage for his donkey? Could Amos have taken Amaziah the Priest to the industrial tribunal in Beth El for wrongful dismissal? How big was the insurance claim by the citizens of Jericho, and did the insurance company refuse to pay on the grounds that it was an 'act of God'?

That is to say, the whole economic substructure of biblical times can potentially put a new perspective on the very questions we ask and the nature of the answers we may reasonably expect to receive.

The breakthrough came with the realization that computers were not being used properly. If you ask only the old questions – how many people wrote Genesis? How many Isaiahs were there? – whatever answer you get, someone is bound to be upset for quite unscientific reasons. And anyway, these matters are nothing that cannot be resolved by someone with a pencil and paper and a lot of patience.

But when the computer is allowed to determine the sort of issues that should be explored, then a whole new statistical science can be created, together with new posts and even departments at universities, and a small sub-industry in more traditional institutions to refute all the results. The Bible is at last beginning to find its true place in the computer age.

But to return to our starting point. In chapter 4 of the Book of Ruth the name of the man who should have redeemed Naomi's property and married Ruth has been suppressed, and instead the anonymous term 'Ploni Almoni' has been substituted. Traditional scholars have thought that this change was done deliberately by the author on religious grounds. Someone not prepared to preserve the name of his kinsman, worried that his own family name might somehow be lost by doing his duty, is punished by having all trace of his name removed. A proper penalty, measure for measure, for his lapse of responsibility.

Such a simplistic explanation, however well-intentioned, could not survive the critical view of a post-Watergate world. The name was removed from the record? Somebody paid!

Why did he want out? He, or at least a later descendant, might just have been embarrassed. How many people, after all, miss the chance to be the great grandfather of King David and the ancestor of the Messiah?

This could certainly explain a low-profile strategy. However, according to a team of scholars in Jerusalem, 'the Religio-Associative and Socio-Historical Increments (RASHI's) do not compute'. They would have us look elsewhere for the motives of the 'pseudo-redeemer' or 'phoney-Almoni'.

At this point, we must state our reservations, on methodological grounds, about their conclusions. We record them only in the interests of the search for objective truth.

For their supposedly new programme under the title 'Polyvalent Socio-Historic Anthropometric Technique' (PSHAT) is really only a thinly disguised attempt to project on to an ancient culture the presuppositions of today, which is clearly inadmissible by any scientific standard.

They conclude that the anonymous redeemer had refused to marry Ruth because of what he considered to be serious irregularities in her conversion, if, indeed, it took place at all through the official ecclesiastical authorities.

We must intrude here an immediate objection. The idea that Elimelech, Naomi's deceased husband, could have countenanced the marriage of his sons to Moabite women without their proper conversion is unthinkable, even if the existence of a competent Beth Din in Moab is hard to prove. And even if, as the text might lead us to believe, he was actually dead at the time of the marriages.

The fact that both his sons dropped dead, while unfortunate, is no proof of divine displeasure, as Job has so competently argued.

But their second theory is as problematical as the first. According to this, it was Ploni's own radical, even reforming, tendencies that led to his downfall, for he queried the formula used in Ruth's conversion affirmation. In accordance with ancient tradition, having married into the Israelite nation out of love for her husband, she quite rightly said 'Your people are my people and your God, my God' (Ruth 1.16).

It is only Ploni's non-Orthodox idea that religious belief should be the only acceptable motive for conversion, and not merely the desire for marriage. Hence his assertion that she should have put 'Your God is my God' first. Once again, however, the flouting of traditional values was punished and he missed the messianic boat.

Feasible as this theory may seem at first glance, even to imagine that there could be religious controversies of this nature in ancient Israel is utterly untenable. Immutable laws, divinely inspired, are not susceptible to such whimsical changes – except at such times as political expedience and, less often, commonsense, intrude. This 'scenario' is too far-fetched.

If the truth must be told, Ploni Almoni may simply have been a racist who wanted nothing to do with a Moabite ('Lest I corrupt my inheritance' Ruth 4.6) and the less we know about him the better.

We are yet again well served by our biblical editors who concealed his identity, even if a few shekels had to change hands somewhere along the line.

BIGTAN AND TERESH

In some ways the Book of Esther seems an ideal subject for a
Purim Spiel. The following is yet another 'go' at biblical scholars,
this time those who start with the assumption that the biblical text
we have today is corrupt and who set about re-writing it. However,
on re-reading some of my arguments here I, too, started believing
the scientific possibilities of my own parody. Now, that's a real
topsy-turvy Purim world!

There are also a couple of sideswipes at 'gematria', (an aramaic
term borrowed from the Greek 'geometry'), which is the Rabbinic
system of adding up the numerical value of the letters of a word
and thence comparing it with similar numbers obtained by adding
up the letters of other words. It has a long and respectable history,
particularly in Jewish mystical thought, but since anything can be
proved to be the numerical equivalent of anything else, by use of
convenient adjustments when they do not exactly fit, it is a
problematic exegetical tool.

Louis Jacobs tells the story of the Rabbi who was asked, 'Why
do we eat *kugel* ('cake', from German via Yiddish, and not
Hebrew at all!) on *Shabbat*?' Came the answer, 'Because the
numerical value of *kugel* is the same as that of *Shabbat*!' However,
if you tot up the letters of *Shabbat* (*shin* = 300, *bet* = 2, *tav* = 400,
giving a total of 702) and compare it with *kugel* (spelling it as *kuf* =
100, *vav* = 6, *gimmel* = 3, *lamed* = 30, giving a total of 139), it is
clear that they do not have the same numerical value at all, and
that *Shabbat* is a far greater number than *kugel*! So what is the
solution? Eat more *kugel*!

On to Bigtan and Teresh.

Though we can accept large parts of the biblical record without
question as the authentic account of events and persons, there are
some sections where we are less certain. This is not because of any
doubts to be cast on the veracity of the anonymous biblical
narrator, but because he, or occasionally she, is citing secondary
materials whose origins are notoriously unreliable.

No better illustration of this exists than the Book of Esther,
which is based on the records preserved in the Chronicles of the
Kings of Persia and Media and the private diaries of Queen
Vashti. Yet it is surprising how uncritical scholars have been about
these materials, given the tendency of royal archives to exaggera-
tion and special pleading.

We can show this point with the two lists of seven names at the beginning of the book which represent respectively the 'eunuchs' (1.10) and the 'princes' (1.14) of King Ahasuerus. We must naturally be suspicious from the very start of the use of the number 'seven', which is an ideal or 'round' number used to indicate the perfection of the system.

A quick check of the names raises a lot of doubts about the legitimacy of these figures. For example in 1.10 we find a 'Binta' (*bet, nun, tav, aleph*), and an 'Avanta' (*aleph, bet, nun, tav, aleph*). Since the only difference between the two is the single letter '*aleph*', they are obviously one and the same person and the name is merely duplicated to change a group of six to the more significant 'seven'.

Likewise in verse 14 we have 'Meres' (*mem, resh, samech*) and 'Mersena' (*mem, resh, samech, nun, aleph*). Here the addition of the '*nun*' as well as an '*aleph*' is clearly a clumsy attempt to confuse the issue, but the gentleman is the same in both cases – once more a mere six people in all.

We can go further. The first eunuch is called 'Mehuman' (*mem, hey, vav, mem, nun*) and it takes no imagination at all to recognize the consonants of the wretched 'Haman' (*hey, mem, nun*) clumsily concealed within it. Indeed, the great mediaeval Jewish exegete, the Magen Ot (Literally, 'The Shielder of the Sign', the title of his lost masterpiece on biblical miracles, of which only three sentences are still extant), of blessed memory, noticed this obvious identification:

Mehuman, that is Haman. And what happened to the missing '*mem*' and '*vav*'? These correspond to the 46 talents of silver Haman had to pay the king for his elevation to high office.

We can discount this clumsy bit of gematria (the numerical value of the letter '*mem*' is 40 and of *vav* is 6) and in many ways it is more wholesome than his spurious attempts to relate the shortening of the name to the losses incurred in the surgical operation that made him a eunuch.

But today we can go beyond even this remarkable insight and cancel out two more names from the cast list of the book. For Bigtan and Teresh, the two who plotted against the king and were overheard and exposed by Mordechai (Esther 2.21–23), are anagrams of names in the lists from chapter 1 we have already mentioned. So that Teresh (*tav, resh, shin*) is the Sheter (*shin, tav, resh*) of 1.14.

Bigtan does not seem to have a corresponding name at first glance, but we are indebted to the three-year-old son of a colleague who spotted that the name Binta, in the eunuch list (1.10), contains '*bet*', '*nun*' and '*tav*' in common with Bigtan.

All that is lacking is the '*gimmel*'. However, if we take the '*aleph*' from the end of Binta and add the two '*alephs*' from the beginning and end of Avanta, whom we have already proved to be the same person, these add up to three seemingly redundant '*alephs*', which, added together, would give us the third letter of the alphabet, the missing '*gimmel*'!

(We are happy to acknowledge our indebtedness to this young scholar who demonstrates so well the value of a sound Jewish education from the earliest years.)

What are we to make of these significant discoveries? First, as we have noted, the king was surrounded by only six people in each of his groups of advisers – the eunuchs who 'prepared his face' (1.10) and the princes who 'looked at his face' (1.14), to use the somewhat picturesque Persian terminology.

Of these, the two conspirators Bigtan and Teresh can be removed, thus reducing the numbers of advisers to five per group. Of these Mehuman gets promoted and renamed Haman, so that there is now a significant imbalance between the two groups. It is into this vacuum that Mordechai steps with his own rapid promotion.

What can we learn from all these calculations? Probably, that the Persian empire under Ahasuerus suffered serious economic difficulties because of his extravagant parties that also tied up most of the ruling classes and bureaucracy for long periods at a time.

Rather than admit the problem publicly, the king, through encouraging or forcing early retirement in some cases, and by physical extermination in others, cut his Cabinet by two-sevenths, thus causing a net saving of some 28.5 per cent on major salaries (more if we note the absence of a need for redundancy payments in some of the above-mentioned cases) while at the same time falsifying the public record.

But the truth will out, however belatedly, and we must be grateful to our Hebrew writer for the meticulous way in which he or she preserved so exactly the documents, leaving it for us to expose this scandalous cover-up, which must be traced all the way up to the throne itself.

Regretfully, we must conclude that Mordechai and Esther would have known this, though we can only speculate on the degree of their complicity. Did they try to pass on the truth to a later generation through recording these names in this way even though prevented from direct intervention in their own time?

We can only speculate, but surely that is the meaning of the very name of the heroine after whom the scroll is called – for the name Esther comes from the root *satar* and means 'I conceal'!

Jonah

Jonah is an inevitable part of a collection like this. The Book of Jonah was one of the first biblical books I studied and I became fascinated both by his character and by the form of the book itself. Why did such a small book (four chapters) produce so many contradictory interpretations? Should we identify with the reluctant prophet, seemingly very narrow in his views, at least according to so many commentaries, or with the author with his magnificent universalism and ironic humour? In the end a study of Jonah became part of my Rabbinic thesis for Ordination at Leo Baeck College, and then the subject of my doctoral dissertation in Heidelberg. The book is still very much part of me – the first introduction for my own students to biblical narrative, as well as the source of discussion on the Day of Atonement when it is the prophetic reading in the afternoon. There is now an extensive commentary on the Book in the High Holyday Prayerbook I co-edited for the Reform Synagogues of Great Britain, and somehow Jonah keeps cropping up in articles, scholarly and otherwise, as well as in innumerable conversations. (I recall a discussion with a politician who told me that he thought the story of Jonah represented every politician's nightmare. The people believed Jonah and repented, and no politician expects to be believed! Moreover, he effectively worked himself out of a job that way.)

So why not a closing chapter on Jonah? And, as befits an ending and a parting, in the form of a meditation.

The Zohar, the central text of Jewish mysticism, speaks of Jonah as follows:

> In the story of Jonah we see the whole of human experience in this world. Jonah descending into the ship is like a human soul that

descends into the world as it enters our body. Why is it called 'Jonah', 'troubled'? Because as soon as it becomes a partner with the body in this world it finds itself full of troubles. For people are in this world as in a ship that is crossing the great ocean and seems to be breaking up.

This troubled and tormented soul on its brief journey through the world is a favoured image of the mediaeval Jewish thinkers. The image begins in the *Sayings of the Fathers* (4.21).

The world is like a corridor to the world to come. Prepare yourself in the corridor so that you may enter the inner chamber.

And it finds one of its most unnerving expressions in the words of the thirteenth-century philosopher, Jedaiah of Beziers:

The world is a tempestuous sea of immense depth and breadth, and time is a frail bridge constructed over it. The beginning of it is fastened with the cords of chaos that preceded existence, while the end of it is to see eternal bliss, and to be enlightened with the light of the King's countenance. The width of the bridge is the width of a human being, and it has no handrail! And you, human creature, against your will are living, and are continually travelling over it, since the day you came to birth.

Beyond the world of physical dangers, where life itself is constantly threatened, there lies the world of the journey of the spirit – a world no less tricky to pass through unharmed. And the soul and body in uneasy alliance must pick their careful way through the two, always running the risk of confusing one with the other or of paying insufficient attention to the legitimate needs and challenges of each. In his book *Awakenings*, Dr Oliver Sacks points to one way in which our confusion may arise:

There is, of course, an ordinary medicine, an everyday medicine, humdrum, prosaic, a medicine for stubbed toes, quinsies, bunions and boils; but all of us entertain the idea of *another* sort of medicine, of a wholly different kind: something deeper, older, extraordinary, almost sacred, which will restore to us our lost health and wholeness, and give us a sense of perfect well-being.

For all of us have a basic, intuitive feeling that once we were whole and well; at least, at peace, at home in the world, totally united with the grounds of our being; and that then we lost this primal, happy, innocent state, and fell into our present sickness

and suffering. We had something of infinite beauty and precious-
ness – and we lost it; we spend our lives searching for what we
have lost; and one day, perhaps, we will suddenly find it. And this
will be the miracle, the millennium!

We may expect to find such ideas most intense in those who are
enduring extremities of suffering, sickness, and anguish, in those
who are consumed by the sense of what they have lost, or wasted,
and by the urgency of recouping before it is too late. Such people,
or patients, come to priests or physicians in desperations of
yearning, prepared to believe anything for a reprieve, a rescue, a
regeneration, a redemption. They are credulous in proportion to
their desperation – the predestined victims of quacks and
enthusiasts.

This sense of what is lost and what must be found, is essentially
a metaphysical one. If we arrest the patient in his metaphysical
search, and ask him *what* it is that he wishes or seeks, he will not
give us a tabulated list of items, but will say, simply, 'My
happiness', 'My lost health', 'My former condition', 'A sense of
reality', 'Feeling fully alive', etc. He does not long for this thing or
that; he longs for a general change in the complexion of things,
for everything to be *all right* again, unblemished, the way it once
was. And it is at this point, when he is searching, here and there,
with so painful an urgency, that he may be led into a sudden
grotesque mistake; that he may (in Donne's words) mistake 'the
Apothecaryes shop' for 'the Metaphorical Deity'; a mistake
which the apothecary or physician may be tempted to encourage.[1]

For us the search for the 'Metaphorical Deity' may seem all to
often a confused and disturbing task, one full of traps no less
dangerous than those awaiting us in the 'Apothecaryes shop'. A
multiplicity of objections, intellectual and emotional, warn us
against the very validity of such a search; and a writer like C. S.
Lewis in *The Screwtape Letters*, has shown us the unengaging
realities of organized religious life that may lead us to reject the very
communities, and their spiritual leaders, who should be offering us
a home in which to make such an exploration. Something stands in
the way – and whether we characterize it as the materialism of the
times we live in, or the workings of some element of our
subconscious, or ascribe it to some externalized principle of evil – all

[1]Oliver Sacks, *Awakenings*, Penguin, revised ed. 1976, pp. 48–9.

too often we give up on the threshold, and settle for the security of a familiar unease, perhaps because we are somehow aware of the risks we run in taking a further step.

This hesitancy is vividly expressed in the Hebrew Bible in stories about the call of prophets to serve God. For them, at least, the source of the call is not questioned and for one of them, Abraham, the response seems to be immediate acquiescence. Yet for others there is a moment of hesitance, expressed in different ways; Moses has a whole string of objections: Who am I to rescue the children of Israel? Anyway they'll never believe You sent me! Anyway I cannot speak adequately! In the end he seems to become quite peevish: 'Oh! send whoever You want!' – anyone, that is, but me (Ex. 4.13). And yet the anger, and perhaps God's anger in reply, is only because he knows that he has swallowed the bait and accepted.

Jeremiah says he is too young (Jer. 1.6). Isaiah feels himself impure (Isa. 6.5). Amos probably complained that he was not professionally qualified (Amos 7.14). Yet in the end, they all had to go.

Leon Roth expressed it well:

It has become fashionable to talk of the relationship between God and man as that of a dialogue. That is as may be; but it should at least be noted that the dialogue involved is not a tea-table conversation. It is rather a call, even a calling to account; and it is curious to observe from the record how some of those called upon found in it terror and suffering and how some, for varying reasons, tried to evade it.[2]

In such a context there is an inevitability to the creation of the Book of Jonah, the story of the prophet who not only refused the call, but went to enormous extremes, to the very brink of death itself, so as to run away from it. Nor do we really know why he refused, for in the typical manner of biblical narratives, we are given a description of events but very little in the way of overt evaluation of why things happened. We, the reader, must follow Jonah on his journey, picking up such clues as we can from what occurs, but ultimately investing the story with our own insights and, inevitably, our own experience and private fears.

The call of God is clear and precise, another task set for one who is used to such things:

[2]Leon Roth, *God and Man in the Old Testament*, Allen & Unwin 1955, p. 19.

Rise, go to Nineveh that great city and call out to them that their evil has come up before Me! (Jonah 1.2).

We know that Jonah is a prophet because he is called such elsewhere in the Bible (II Kings 14.25). But he is not named as one in our book, and in fact the whole tenor of the story is to make him into an everyman, not bound by time or space. Yet Nineveh is a real place – the capital of the Assyrian Empire, a military power that cast its shadow of fear across the entire Near East. To the Assyrians goes the credit of inventing the military tactic of uprooting entire populations, settling them elsewhere and replacing them with other defeated peoples. The tactic was to prove successful in destroying the Northern Kingdom of Israel, and leading, incidentally, to the legend-inspiring ten lost tribes. Nineveh, for Jonah, was the Berlin of the Third Reich. To Nineveh he is sent, but to Tarshish he flees.

If we can identify the place accurately, it is somewhere at the southern tip of Spain, that is to say not merely in the diametrically opposite direction from Nineveh, but literally across the sea at the other end of the world. Not only is it a journey into the unknown, and into considerable danger, but the economics of it must have presented a problem! Certainly on the basis of this account the Rabbis assumed that the prophets must have been wealthy, arguing, from a precise reading of the Hebrew text, that Jonah hired the entire boat for his exclusive use! (He paid 'it's' fare and not just 'his' fare (1.3).)

To flee from God, Jonah must have sold up his home, left everything behind and set off at the risk of his life. To flee from God, he reproduces the experience of the patriarchs, of ancient Israel and of the Jewish people, of going into exile, but this time against the will of God. Yet the author hints that his flight is more than just an attempt to escape the immediate task. Three times the Hebrew verb for 'going down' (*yarad*) occurs in the first chapter – as Jonah goes down to Jaffa, and into the boat (v. 3), then down into the innermost part of the boat to sleep (v. 5) – and then a fourth time, because of a pun in the Hebrew text, when he goes down into a deep sleep (*vayeiradam*). There is a direction in his journey – into unconsciousness as he sleeps through the storm, and ultimately into oblivion, as he asks to be thrown overboard. Jonah in flight is on a journey away from God, on a journey towards death.

But the prophet is not alone on his travels. Others are borne along, and others are thus exposed to the danger he seems to think is merely his private concern. The sailors are characterized as people of remarkable sensitivity and generosity. When the storm threatens to destroy them, they pray to their respective gods. They then apply standard 'technological' ploys to discover the culprit, by casting lots and the lot falls on Jonah. Instead of throwing him overboard at once, they open up a court of law and ply Jonah with questions trying to establish his identity. What is he running from? Of what is he guilty? When Jonah, having admitted his responsibility, is asked what should be done, he has the chance to ask to be taken back, but he refuses – so the sailors try to row him back, but no one can make that return on behalf of another. When finally defeated, they turn to God:

> We beg you, Eternal, let us not perish for this man's life, and do not hold us guilty of shedding innocent blood, for You are the Eternal, as You will it, so You act (1.14).

They are trapped in a 'double bind'; to do nothing means they will drown with Jonah; to throw him overboard means they are guilty of murder and thus condemned to death. Only God can untangle such a paradox. So Jonah's solution of self-immolation is not simply a generous gesture to save the lives of his fellows – otherwise he only needed to jump overboard without involving them at all. So death seems to be the logical conclusion of his flight, and the sailors count for very little; they can only be on the periphery of his concerns.

The Rabbis, however, recognized their worth, and portrayed them as making yet one more bid to save the prophet. First they lowered him till his feet entered the water. At once the sea calmed down – so they hauled him back aboard, but the storm raged again. Again they lowered him to his waist, again calm, and again they pulled him back. But the storm returned. The third time he went in up to his neck before the cycle was repeated. In the end they had no choice and threw him in.

The author has twice recorded their growing fear as the storm increased against them (1.5, 10). But their fear is now greatest with the calm that descends – for their fear has become the fear and awe of God (1.16). They made sacrifices and vowed vows – and the Rabbis had them returning to Jerusalem where they converted to the faith in the one God. Even on his flight, Jonah serves God's purposes.

We may also read this story inside out – for how do we come to recognize that our journey is actually a flight? Perhaps in the damage we do to others on the way, if the realization ever penetrates to our awareness.

Certainly for Jonah other messages were continually coming through. In one of the most subtle ploys of the author, the words of the captain to Jonah when he asks him to rise up and call on his God (1.6) are identical with the words of God's call. For the captain they merely mean: 'Wake up and pray!' For Jonah the words of God echo in the air waiting for him to respond. Thus the captain becomes the unconscious messenger of God's word, and indeed the wind, the storm, as later on the fish, the gourd, the worm, all of nature, become the agents of God, bringing the divine word to the recalcitrant prophet.

Psalm 139.7 reads 'Whither can I go from Your *spirit*?' But the word for 'spirit', (*ruach*), can also be translated literally as 'wind' – the wind that brings the storm to the sea, the wind that will affect Jonah sitting beneath the remains of his hut, the wind that is part of a creation faithfully serving its master. Or is this just the nightmare in which Jonah finds himself trapped, a paranoid universe in which every person, every sound, each breath of wind, closes in on him with some message he does not wish to hear. For Jonah in flight, even death seems to be the better option than living with the God who haunts him. But even the luxury of death is not permitted him – waiting in the wings is the fish.

A century ago scholars still tried to identify the precise fish that swallowed Jonah – not a whale but some sort of shark seems to have been favoured. Today it is hard to discuss the remarkable creature as anything but a symbolic womb. And yet it is worth noting the function it plays for the author. Most obviously it gets Jonah out of the sea and back to dry land. It also provides him a home for three days in which to reassess his situation. In fact the Rabbis were rather annoyed at Jonah for taking so long to come out with his prayer.

They composed a fascinating account of what happened during this period on the basis of a change in the grammatical form of the word in the Hebrew for the fish that occurs between verses 1 and 2. This change could imply that between the two verses the fish changed from a male to a female. Hence they constructed a long underwater voyage taken by Jonah in which he visited the foundations of the earth, the path through the Sea of Reeds taken by the children of Israel on leaving Egypt – and generally exploring significant moments in Israel's divine history. God grew so impatient at this Cook's tour that he sent a female fish to threaten Jonah's male transporter, and the latter vomited Jonah out into the jaws of the former. It was only in the discomfort of this new accommodation, jostled on all sides by embryo fish that Jonah finally felt the need to pray to God!

And even then the Rabbis were not satisfied with his actual prayer as recorded in the Bible (2.3–10) because there is no hint in it of Jonah repenting or otherwise apologizing for his flight from God in the first place.

Was Jonah's time in the fish one of those transforming experiences? Did he emerge with a new heightened consciousness or at least a greater insight into his situation and his nature? Again, conventional psychology would probably say yes. Surely such an experience – a regression to the womb, the dark night of the soul, sensory deprivation – must have done something to him. And yet – there is a stubborn obliviousness about Jonah that is hearteningly consistent. True, he prays. But the psalm he recites[3] is remarkable for all that is left out.

In its outer edges it says quite bluntly to God – You threw me in (v. 4) and You pulled me out (v. 7), with not a word about how this came about. More sensitive is the play on Jonah's gradual physical descent ('The waters closed in over me; the deep was round about me, weeds wrapped over my head, I went down to the base of the mountains . . .' (2.6–7) which is matched by a spiritual rise. Whereas at the beginning he says:

I am driven out of Your sight, yet still I will look to Your holy Temple (2.5).

At the end, when he again speaks of God's holy Temple, the wording is quite different:

When my soul was fainting within me, it was the Eternal that I remembered, and my prayer reached out to You, to Your holy Temple (2.8).

---

[3]Scholars have long debated whether Jonah's prayer in chapter 2 was an original part of the book or a later addition. The arguments (that it does not seem to fit as Jonah is not yet saved, that there is no mention of repentance, that it is poetry while the rest of the book is prose (sic!)) can all be countered, and more recent trends in scholarship have asserted its legitimacy. Certainly, as the book now stands, it forms an integral part and must be interpreted accordingly.

What gets lost in the translation is the emphatic 'I' that comes to
the fore in the Hebrew of Jonah's prayer. In verse 5 it is a strong:
'And as for me, I said . . . ' with the implication that Jonah
considered himself still the master of the situation. Yet as he sinks
lower and lower into the depths (another phase of the 'descent' that
began in chapter 1) something happens to him. In the matching first
person statement in verse 8, as he faints away, the 'I' disappears
completely, and a disembodied prayer manages to reach the
Temple of God, stripped of all pride and egoism. Jonah has indeed
undergone some change of perspective – for one brief moment his
centre has moved outside his limited self and located itself within
the Temple of God. But it becomes rapidly reconstituted two verses
later at the conclusion (v. 10) where, in an echo of a standard
thanksgiving psalm, Jonah says:

And as for me, I will sacrifice to You with thankful voice; what I
have vowed I will fulfil.

The 'I' is restored, as indeed it must be, as Jonah moves back
from the fish to the outer world.

And yet what has really changed? There is a puzzling beginning to
chapter 3 where we read:

The word of the Eternal came to Jonah a second time (3.1).

There then follows virtually the identical message (certainly the
three words of his call reappear) as we had in chapter 1.

Why must God repeat the divine command if Jonah has now
become reconciled to his task? Presumably the answer lies in the
closing statement of Jonah's prayer that we have just read. For in his
moment of dutiful piety, Jonah has just made an oath to head for
Jerusalem and make sacrifices and fulfil vows, presumably intoning
the words of the thanksgiving psalm he has just composed. Surely
this is the pious step he should now undertake. No! says God. There
is still a task awaiting you in Nineveh, and that is where you should
be heading!

For Jonah the retreat into piety is yet another evasion of the call
from God. When flight from God does not work, there is always
flight to God, or to that convenient God who makes no demands
beyond those the worshipper can comfortably offer.

This evaluation of Jonah's piety may seem harsh – but it may be
backed by one other ironic touch that underlies the same theme.
Jonah ends his prayer on a triumphant note: *yeshuatah ladonay*,

'Salvation belongs to the Eternal!' For God has heard his prayer and God has saved him. And indeed God hears, and speaks to the fish, and with a fine sensitivity to the ambiguity of Jonah's confession of faith, the fish vomits him out!

In chapter 3, after bringing Jonah reluctantly into Nineveh – it takes three days to cover the city, Jonah travels for only one day (compare 3.3 and the beginning of 3.4) – the story turns to the actions of the Ninevites. It starts with a ground swell of public feeling: the people fast and put on sackcloth and ashes, the traditional response to threatened disaster. The news reaches the king who in turn removes his robes, dons sackcloth and sits in ashes. Finally, by decree of the king, all are commanded to fast and don sackcloth, human beings and animals alike.

There would seem to be here a certain degree of repetition and, indeed, redundancy, in this threefold description of sackcloth and fasting. However the author has been building a rising tide of activity as a jumping off point for the king's final command. For till now these actions are part of a conventional response to danger, which indeed the repetition firmly establishes. With the king's closing words, we leap into a totally new dimension:

> And let everyone turn from their evil way, and from the violence of their hands. Who knows, God may turn and relent, and turn back from God's fiery anger, so that we perish not (3.8–9).

With these words, borrowed from the Book of Jeremiah (compare Jer. 26.3, 13, 19), and thus bearing an added ironic edge in the mouth of a pagan king, the response of the Ninevites moves out of the area of fatalism into the realm of moral choice. Indeed, as the Rabbis pointed out, God does not respond in the story to their sackcloth and ashes but instead:

> And God saw their actions, how they turned from their evil ways, and God relented of the evil God had said to do to them (3.10).

As the chapter is constructed, we have here a stepwise build-up of activity ending with the breakthrough to the new dimension of religious hope – and there at the peak, God is waiting. In our previous chapter, as Jonah sinks lower and lower, he too breaks through to a new experience of God – there at the lowest reach of hopelessness and despair, God is waiting to meet him. The two chapters form mirror images of each other, and yet again we are reminded of lines from Psalm 139 (v. 8):

> If I rise up to heaven – there, You!
> If I make the underworld my bed – behold, You!

In this joyful affirmation that God is to be found, even at the very extremes of existence, in exaltation or in despair, there comes to mind the famous song of the Hasidic master, Levi Yitzchak of Berditchev – the 'Dudele'.

> Where I wander – You!
> Where I ponder – You!
> Only You, You again, always You!
> You! You! You!
> When I am gladdened – You!
> When I am saddened – You!
> Only You, You again, always You!
> You! You! You!
> Sky is You, earth is You!
> In every trend, at every end,
> Only You, You again, always You!
> You! You! You!

So the centre of our book pivots around this ladder leading into the depths and the heights. In chapter one we have had enormous activity as Jonah fled, in the closing chapter, on the surface at least, we have a moment of stillness – for Jonah sits and sits and sits.

Jonah takes his place outside Nineveh, knowing that the people have repented, yet nevertheless hoping for, and indeed willing, God to destroy it anyway. His is not the stillness of acceptance, of harmony, of reconciliation, for Jonah rages. There is even an ironic overtone to the picture of Jonah's position. For within the city the king in sackcloth sits in ashes in great discomfort praying for the city to be saved; while without, Jonah sits in reasonable comfort beneath his shelter, praying for the city to be destroyed.

Why is Jonah angry? First, we should note another exquisite touch of the author in presenting Jonah's second prayer in the book (4.2–3). Jonah begins with the conventional terminology of prayer – the same, in fact, used by the sailors in chapter 1. 'I beg You, Eternal . . .' and at the end he will use the same form of request – an imperative softened by the added 'I beg You':

So now, O Eternal, I beg You, take my life from me, for it is better for me to die than to live.

But between these two expressions, there bursts through all the resentment he has bottled up inside since the beginning of this absurd mission:

Did I not say just this while I was still on my own land? That is why I tried first to flee to Tarshish, for I know that You are a gracious and merciful God, slow to anger, generous in love, who relents from punishing!

Jonah is here quoting the list of God's qualities first revealed to Moses (Ex. 34.6–7), God's compassion and mercy, love for humanity and enduring patience in the face of their wrongdoing. But Jonah is spitting them out into God's face – I knew You'd end up forgiving them, and You shouldn't!

That at least is Jonah's overt argument. But what he actually objects to is still a matter of conjecture. Some feel that Jonah is a nationalist who does not wish to see the enemy Nineveh go unpunished, perhaps in anticipation of the destruction they will bring to the Northern Kingdom – this would make Jonah a heroic patriot, prepared to die so as to save his people. Others extend the sentiment but in a negative way, and see in Jonah an expression of a narrow particularism that resented the idea that God's love could be extended to people beyond Israel's borders. Others see Jonah as a champion of rigid justice, offended by God's softness on evildoers. One might go further and see Jonah as someone who wishes the universe to be governed by clear, unambiguous rules, wherein there is the security of knowing that action A will lead to consequence B with no random factor, like God's seemingly anarchic love, to confuse the system. All these are possible elements in Jonah's viewpoint, and yet behind them there remains the deeper question of the tension between the private, limited ego of human beings and the will of God, in whatever form and with whatever terminology we envisage this interaction.

Throughout the story we have seen this confrontation: God hurled a wind on to the sea; Jonah went down to sleep through the subsequent storm.[4] God says Nineveh will not be destroyed; Jonah

[4]Most translations read the end of 1.5 as a 'pluperfect' – 'Jonah had already gone down into the ship'. They would appear to be influenced by the assumption that during such a storm, Jonah is highly unlikely to be able to go down into the ship to

wills that it should be, and will sit there till it happens. In this final
chapter, the author even organizes the conversation so that words
match words, actions match actions, as the two protagonists
confront each other. In the Hebrew text the identical number of
words are given to Jonah's great speech of complaint at the
beginning (4.2–3) and to God's long speech of explanation at the
end (4.10–11). And God finally spells out their point of difference,
again by using personal pronouns to give an emphatic form of
expression to both of the 'characters':

> As for you, you felt pity for the gourd . . . As for Me, should I not
> feel pity for Nineveh . . .

Again, as Leon Roth put it, the call of God is a calling to account.
The God from whom Jonah cannot flee demands that he confront
the very problem he wishes to avoid.

There follow in the rest of the story more magical stage effects. The
great fish gives way in turn to a magical plant, a destructive worm
and a harsh wind. The violence of the storm is replaced by the
violence of nature, creation and destruction, growth and struggle.
And the outer violence is matched by a whole range of inner
emotions that grip Jonah. Leaving the city he rages; under the shade
of God's plant he rejoices greatly, both for the shade and the
apparent evidence of God's favour; then the sun beats upon his
head, as he too experiences the destructive power he would so
happily have unleashed on Nineveh, and in despair he asks for
death. Again the author uses the device of repetition to indicate a
change in perspective. Early in the chapter Jonah wished to die in
angry defence of his attitude to God's unacceptable behaviour
(4.3): he would give his life for a principle. But at the end it is the

---

sleep. But the grammar of the Hebrew (as in the identical structure in the previous
verse where it says 'The Eternal hurled a great wind into the sea') allows it to be read
as a simple continuity of what was going on. Indeed that was Jonah's deliberate
response to God's actions – God challenged him with the storm, Jonah turned his
back and went to bed! Should it be argued that it is difficult to sleep through such a
storm, I have it on good authority from a colleague that it is possible. When caught in
a yacht in a gale, he and his friends, aware there was nothing they could possibly do,
and that they would either survive or not, strapped themselves into their bunks, took
a bottle of whiskey each and slept it out.

physical discomfort that again (4.8) leads him to make the same request, and here we have a clue to the whole curious episode with the gourd.

In a final challenge, God asks about Jonah's feelings for the gourd: 'though you neither laboured over it nor made it grow'. The gourd served Jonah, he had some relationship to it, though perhaps God is being ironic in suggesting Jonah felt pity for it. But God could equally have used a pet animal or any other creature for this illustration if the only point to be made here was that Jonah could feel something for another part of creation. Why the gourd?

The answer seems to lie in the solution to another problem that has worried scholars. If Jonah has already built himself a booth beneath which to shelter from the sun, what is the purpose of the gourd, and indeed what happens to the booth? Presumably both are swept away by the wind, leaving Jonah exposed, but why this seeming repetition?

While Jonah is angry with God and enters into a theological debate about the nature of God's qualities, he has incidentally done something else. In verse 5 Jonah has gone out of the city and sat down to await events. But the sentence then adds that he got up again and built himself a shelter and sat again beneath it so as to watch the imminent, hoped-for destruction in comfort. It is at this point that God, as if saying, 'we have run out of words with which to talk to each other,' picks up Jonah's actions and responds in the same way. God appears to be saying: 'You may think that you are somehow acting out of righteous anger, but perhaps really at the heart of the matter, is your concern for your own comfort. Very well, if it is shade that you wish, shade you shall have, the most wondrous shade you could imagine – and with that physical aspect we shall continue our debate.' So the gourd becomes the logical element which God brings to bear, and with which to make the final point.[5]

Nineveh is saved because of God's patience. No less wondrous is God's patience with the reluctant prophet, a patience that goes

---

[5] This view is reinforced by a word play in the text. Jonah builds his booth to sit *batzel*, 'in the shade'. The purpose of the gourd (v. 6) is explicitly twofold: *lih'yot tzel al rosho l'hatzil lo mera'ato*, 'to be *shade* upon his head to 'deliver' him from his evil/anger'. The word for 'deliver' comes from an entirely different verbal root from the word for 'shade', but in this grammatical form provides a masterful word-play (*lih'yot tzel/l'hatzil lo*). We might translate: 'To be a *shade* upon his head to help him *shed* his anger'.

beyond the confines of the book. For though the religious traditions try to supply an affirmative answer to God's final question to Jonah, the Bible story wisely ends without it. We do not know if Jonah has a change of heart, if he is convinced by God's argument. We do not even know if this extraordinary man who has been subjected to the most intensive series of experiences, emerges at the end any different from before. We want to think he has, because religious and healing professions alike need the myth that human nature is changeable; that repentenace, insight, growth, whatever terminology we use, are available and that we, the practitioners, can somehow help bring them about. But perhaps it is refreshingly necessary to encounter a Jonah once in a while, who asserts the right to remain stiffnecked, blind and wilful, despite the most frenzied efforts of others to persuade or even force such a person to change. But that is a whimsical aside. For whether Jonah changes or not, it seems that he cannot ever escape the call to change that set him off on his adventures in the first place.

For the psalmist, as we have seen, the universal presence of God is a matter of wonder; for Levi Yitzchak of Berditchev, a source of joy; but for Jonah it is a paranoiac's nightmare. Whatever our response, there is no neutral ground.

> For people are in this world as in a ship that is crossing the great ocean and seems to be breaking up.

For Jonah, the search for security leads him to close off this threatening outside world, with its peoples, friend and foe alike, and its multiplicity of creatures all of which demand his attention and concern. But God would have him meet the other, perhaps because the security Jonah seeks is a myth and no solution to the problem of living. Perhaps that is the idea behind the cryptic remark of the Hasidic master, Nachman of Bratzlav. He too speaks about the narrow path we tread during the brief time given us on earth:

> This entire world is but a narrow bridge – but the essential thing is never to be afraid.